BEING BAD

BREAKING THE RULES AND
BECOMING EVERYTHING YOU'RE
NOT SUPPOSED TO BE

ARIELLE EGOZI

CHRONICLE PRISM

An Acknowledgment:

In writing about oneself, other people become characters in the story. There are always multiple perspectives besides one's own, and what I've written here is mine. Some names have been changed or omitted, to protect privacy.

Portions of the chapter "Bad Daughter" were originally published as "I Am Jewish. But I'm Also Latina" in *Hey Alma*. May 31, 2023.

Library of Congress Cataloging-in-Publication Data available.

ISBN 978-1-7972-2897-6

Manufactured in the United States of America.

Design by Pamela Geismar, Domino Design.
Typeset in Alda OT, Trade Gothic, and Pink Sugar.

10 9 8 7 6 5 4 3 2 1

CHRONICLE PRISM

Chronicle Prism is an imprint of Chronicle Books LLC, 680 Second Street, San Francisco, California 94107

www.chronicleprism.com

To every kid who's ever felt alone, ugly, or wrong.
We aren't these things. We never were.

And to David, my jaguar in the sky.

"What I'm writing to you is not for reading—
it's for being."

—*Clarice Lispector*

My love language is . . . all of them.

I had to make you a little present too.

Pretend I've wrapped it up in a box as a love letter.
I'm so grateful you're here.

Unwrap it when you're alone in your room and cozy
under some covers:

www.arielleegozi.com/beingbad

*It'll ask for your email not to be creepy,
just to send you the goodies :)

CONTENTS

If for whatever reason you pick up this book then put it down again, just remember this:

You deserve to be wholly,

fully,

completely,

strangely,

and gorgeously

yourself.

That's the only secret to being bad.

INTRODUCTION

> "So it turned out that power was the quality
> of knowing what you liked. An odd thing for
> power to be."
>
> —*Eve Babitz*

A weird thing happened last summer.

Headlines all over the world, in every language from Hindi to Icelandic, bore my name. My inboxes were suddenly filled with the biggest media publications in the world reaching out for interviews, radio stations and podcasts wanting sound bites, and producers wanting to cast me in shows and documentaries about my life. I also got *hundreds* of messages from strange men—either soliciting my sexual services or damning me for them.

I've been writing for over a decade and speaking on stages around the world for years—I'm "nichely" famous in certain spaces—but the virality of what happened in the summer of 2022 was the accidental catapult beyond that niche and into a worldwide conversation.

When I listed "sex work" as a LinkedIn work experience, it wasn't for press, money, or any kind of fame, but to simply take another step closer to myself. A lot of the world didn't like it, and some of the world did. Either way, it doesn't matter. I wasn't doing it for anyone but myself.

This is a book about what it takes to break ground, which is really just what it takes to be yourself.

It's about all the tiny steps that lead to bigger ones, and how we all deserve to make an imprint on the world in our own way. You don't have to be in any headlines or streaming your story on Netflix, but the more space you make for yourself in your own life, the more space everyone around you can make for themselves too. I'm writing this book because I want more space for all the pieces of myself, and I want to make more space for all the pieces of you too.

I've spent my life shape-shifting to fit in with the world around me. I come from immigrants, and this is what immigrant families do. To stick out is a death sentence—literally. So we bend and morph and twist ourselves depending on the people, the place, the purpose.

We always know how to get what we need, *even if that comes at the expense of what we want.*

My family has had to start over every generation. It's not

hyperbole, and it's not an exaggeration. The cycle goes like this: We're kicked out of where we live, we leave everything behind, and we adopt the new ways of life from the country we resettle in. Generations of my family have coped this way, and to their success. My abuelo's company was the first Latino-owned organization to go public on the American Stock Exchange. My last name has made history many times. I am proud of the strength, creativity, and honor that is placed on it by anyone who knows our story. But for most of my life, I felt enormous pressure to cope the way my ancestors had. I am the first in my family to be born in America, and what was expected of me was nothing less than to fulfill the American Dream. After all, a lot was given up for the possibility. A lot was sacrificed for the chance.

But ultimately, rather than the American Dream my parents and grandparents wanted, I want to get what *I* want, not what anyone else has outlined for me.

Instead of setting my sights on what success looks like in America, I've chosen to grapple with what success looks like to me. Underneath all the different cultures and countries my family has adopted, I want to know who I am and why.

This separates me not only from those who share a different ancestral story, but from my own ancestors as well. Their support hasn't always been present on my journey, and many of their blessings have been revoked. They don't understand why I must be *public* with my ideas, let alone say them out loud. They don't understand that for me, the American Dream doesn't have to be making and selling shoes like theirs had to be, or being a doctor (or married to one) like they could only once have dreamed; they don't understand that instead, they've given me the chance to achieve the biggest American Dream of all—the chance to live a life where I get to choose to be myself.

My family has never been wanted by any country we've entered. In fact, we were already rejected once by America, which is how some of us ended up in Cuba. Close, but not quite.

When we did come to America, we weren't allowed to enter certain places because we were Jewish. Because we were Cuban. Because we were both. Next-door neighbors yelled at us every night to go back to our country. Restaurants in certain parts of town wouldn't let us in. My grandfather's multimillion-dollar company? No law firm would work with him to help file for an IPO because he was a brown Jew employing thousands of refugees.

We figured it out. We always do.

That's the part that's in my body; that's the part that's in my genes. And that's the part I want to offer you in this book.

I'm a refugee of my own history because my story isn't wanted there, so I'm now starting over just like my ancestors did. Except this time, I'm not entering someone else's country. I'm mapping out an entirely new compass, a new structure, a new set of rules. It's a place where all are welcome, as long as you welcome everyone else. It's a place where bodies are honored and voices are heard. It's a place where eating a cookie for breakfast is encouraged and wearing a feather boa to dinner is common. It's a place that always has space for you and doesn't ask you to be any other way than how you are. It's a place to rest, a place to dance, a place to come home. It's a place to be bad.

This is a book about being bad.

It's a book for lifelong people pleasers ready to retire, for those who are skeptical of anything "set in stone." It's for folks who've already diverged from society's expectations, and for all those who are still longing to do so. This is for the brave and the curious, the shamed and the shunned who are now finally ready to shine.

This book is about doing the opposite of what's expected from you and listening to yourself instead of anyone else. It's about waking up to your body and using it as a tool to listen to your intuition. It's about dusting off all the shit that's accumulated on top of you from generations past and making space for what *you* want, for what *you* are. It's about trusting yourself.

The words in these pages are a reclamation, a process of externalizing all the things I kept inside of me. This is how I saved myself, and I hope it inspires you to externalize too. To realize all the ways you've been made to believe you're wrong, to dig them out, look at them, and SAY THEM OUT LOUD. To not keep them in, to not believe they're yours.

It's a refusal of external pressure and a celebration of internal resilience. It's a deconstruction of what you thought about your own identity and your relationship to yourself and to the world. It's a coming home to everything that's underneath—the strength, the joy, the *power* that is simply you being you.

In this book I talk a lot about power—something that can be hard to see with the eye but is somehow quite tangible enough to touch. Power can't exist on its own—it's a state that's forever in relation to another. Power is a dynamic, a fluid conversation between parties. There is always a giving and a receiving, an exchange. It's not static; rather, it exists as a wave, the convex and the concave.

So too is the relationship we have to ourselves. It shifts with context, with emotion, with our environment. It's never static. To believe otherwise is to give all our power away.

I used to live in the prison of people-pleasing, and what's in this book has been the key to my escape. I now spend my days relishing the freedom outside of it; not only is it a lot more fun, but I also get a lot more done. I put myself first and know I don't have to suffer to make others more comfortable or to convince anyone of my worth.

Neither do you.

So I'm going to be as honest as I can be in these pages, but no more honest than that. I'm going to be as open as I can be, but no more open than that.

I can't give to you what I still can't give to myself. But I'm working on it.

As you read these pages, know that I am no expert. For years people have given me all sorts of names and titles, especially in relation to humans, relationships, and sex. Yeah, I think about these things and read about them a lot more than most people, but it's really only because I live any of it that I choose to speak to it.

Because I can't speak to what I haven't experienced. I can't speak to what I don't know. Even all the things I do know, I only know for myself. I don't know them for you.

So anything and everything I say in here, question it. Toss it around in your mind for a while. Don't make it yours unless it already is. My hope is that this moment in my journey can exist as a reminder for you, something to hold on to when things get extra hard, extra confusing, extra unclear.

It doesn't have to be anything more than that, but maybe, it can be.

GIRL

"Her first step is to take inventory [. . .]. She puts history through a sieve, winnows out the lies, looks at the forces that we as a race, as women, have been a part of [. . .]. She reinterprets history and, using new symbols, she shapes new myths."

—*Gloria Anzaldúa*

I didn't know who Frida Kahlo was until I was at university, sitting in the library and flipping through a book on twentieth-century surrealist painters.

This was right before her face, stone-cold and stoic, would be plastered across notebooks, water bottles, and pencil cases in every color.[1]

Despite being turned into late-capitalist faux-feminist fodder, I owe a lot to this artist, a woman—a queer one—who wore her dark hair twisted in braids with a singular eyebrow slashed across her face like a sword. A symbol of softness and of strength.

I have an eyebrow just like hers, and when I was younger, I hated it.

As the oldest child whose needs seemed to be forever invisible to my parents, I couldn't wait any longer for them to notice

---

1   Surely even the ashes of this militant anti-commercial communist woman are displeased about that.

it. I'd waited patiently for the hairs on my legs and under my arms to curl long enough for my mother to see them so she'd get me a razor ("*mi amor*, they're *so long!*"). I was mortified to ask to be taken to the drugstore to buy deodorant, and I was the last girl in middle school whose mom bought her a bra. I was caught between the desperation of wanting to be seen and the desperation of wanting to become invisible once I was. Either way, I wasn't planning on processing any of that before I did something about my unibrow.

I knew how to shave my legs—how much different could it be to shave my face?

One morning before school, I looked in the mirror and decided it was time. It was the ugliest thing I'd ever seen, this weird caterpillar crawling across my skin. It bugged me that hair had just *decided* to grow there. I felt out of control, vulnerable to its whims, its patterns. It was the early 2000s and thin eyebrows were everything and everywhere. Mine were dark and full, framing my eyes in an obvious way. I hated them.

My body was changing, and I was starting to get an overwhelmingly uncomfortable amount of attention from the boys at school, and I didn't want to give them something to make fun of. They liked me, so they looked at me, which meant they had a habit of using their gaze to slice into me—"positive" or negative, it was never for my benefit, as if they were getting back at me for holding this weird power over them that I'd never asked for.

I took the razor, so pink I could've licked it, and sliced my eyebrow in half. I took the blades flat down the center of my forehead and exhaled in pleasure. How wonderful it felt to make a choice over my own body.

I looked at myself again in the mirror, proudly. The fur in the middle of my forehead was gone. It was smooth, gorgeous, and clean. I now had two eyebrows instead of one . . . but an entire half of one of them was missing, torn off, gone.

Oh no. Oh no no no.

I had five minutes before I had to leave for school. I dropped the razor, the rubber grip bouncing on the bathroom floor as I tried to give myself bangs, do a side part, figure out what I needed to do to hide this horrible mistake.

At school I hoped that, by some miracle, no one would notice. Half a day went by and I started to relax, thinking my mistake had been overlooked by my peers.

Until one of the guys in my grade, the class clown who was always making jokes about my boobs, called my name behind me in the courtyard.

"Hey, Arielle—what happened to your face?"

"What are you talking about?" I asked innocently, turning around to face him, my eyes training on the ground the whole time.

"Something's weird with your face."

If I didn't look at him, I was invisible. I could disappear. He wouldn't be able to see me. He, of all people, couldn't know the truth. He'd tell everyone.

"It's . . . your eyebrows. Your eyebrows are weird." He stepped closer, looking past my perfectly placed curtain of hair into my forehead. His eyes widened. "Did you shave them?"

"*What?*" I said incredulously. "No."

Deny, deny, deny.

"Yeah, you did," he started laughing. "They look so weird."

"I think *I* would know if I shaved them or not. I didn't do anything to them. This is just how they *are*." I stomped off to the bathroom and cried.

I had made all this effort to hide the bigness of my eyebrows, and instead I had brought them even more attention.

I thought I'd never be able to admit what I had done. This was the first time I had ever lied, and I was broken over it. I felt so much shame—not because I had given myself half an eyebrow, but because I had *made a choice* to change something about myself. It felt silly. It felt self-involved. It felt wrong. It seemed to validate that this simple act of "defiance"—letting *myself* make decisions about my body at twelve years old, instead of my parents, the boys at school, the magazines, and everyone else who seemed to have opinions about it—was a slippery slope into the dark world of vanity, lying, and betrayal. I felt sick.

I had no idea how long eyebrows took to grow back, but anything longer than *immediately* was too long.

I came home and my mom laughed at me. Later, she had friends over and she called me out of my room to say hi.

She didn't introduce me. All she said was, "Look at what she did to her eyebrows!" Her laughter, which we almost never got to hear anymore since her divorce, filled the whole house.

Eventually they grew back, and eventually I learned how to use tweezers. I still felt guilty about plucking them, this weird feeling like I was lying to everyone, hiding something from them by taking the hair away. A decade later, full eyebrows became popular again, and everyone who had previously sported thin ones started tattooing hairs on their face to fill them out.

How fickle beauty is, I thought. I had spent my life wishing for something different, hoping for thin blond brows that weren't mine, and could never be, to frame my face, and now that "exoticism" was popular, people were paying thousands of dollars to look like me.

As an adult, I stopped plucking my unibrow. I let it grow out. The fur was tender to me now, a reminder of how I'd been taught to hate something of mine that had always simply, and stubbornly, been. It was also a reminder of my shame. How easy it was to feel ashamed when I was trying to be something I wasn't. How easy it was to feel ashamed when I believed I had to ask permission to make choices over my own body. How easy it was to feel ashamed when I'd been brave, and vulnerable, and failed anyway.

It wasn't illegal to have eyebrows that connected, and yet it felt hugely political to just allow them to be that way.

Today, no one pays attention to my connected eyebrow. I forget that it's there too. But every once in a while, when I'm deep in thought, or just wanting to share a tender moment with myself, I'll run my fingers down the center of my forehead—my third eye, my unibrow—and come back to my center, come back to myself. The power that no one, and no razor, can ever take away.

Frida knew this, and now, so do I.

We're all born into inherent wrongness. No one is exempt.

Based on a body part (or lack of a body part), life in our society is mapped out for us—our interests, our desires, whom we should love, how we should live, what we should wear.

For those of us born with a vulva, that journey is expected to bring us to our destination: being a good girl so that, one day, we might grow up to be a good woman. Each of us has been sold a slightly different story about what makes a girl *good*. It might mean following instructions (our father's; later, our husband's) or always wearing a smile. It might mean not sleeping around, or just as important, knowing when to stay quiet (most of the time).

Regardless, there are three things about good girls that are *always* true.

(1) Good girls don't exist, so, (2) we will *all* ultimately fail to be good, which (3) hurts.

The fact remains that even in our current postmodern stage of a "post-woke" world, the way we simply *are*—the way we move, talk, walk, sit, think, express, and love—can still be considered "wrong" depending on what body we're in. No one asks any of us what *we* might like to wear, who or what *we* might desire, or how *we* would like to be.

There's already rules for that, and we're just supposed to follow them. All of us are essentially set up to chase fake versions of ourselves, fitting into the behaviors, desires, and actions that are chosen for us way before we ever figured out which gender we even wanted *to be*. Instead of being born into a world where we have the full capacity and limitless potential and space to just

become
who
we
are

—and have *that* be good, and whole, and worthy, and accepted—

we're born into a world where simply by sitting with our legs spread, talking too much with our hands, or wearing an outfit that dips too low, we are, already, *bad.*

By simply being ourselves, we are wrong.

Remember that feeling of glittering power in early childhood, before we believed we were rotten and shameful and we just believed we were absolutely incredible?

As a kid in the early '90s, I refused to wear anything that wasn't a plastic sparkling heel. My buttons were all plastic pearl roses, and all my socks were trimmed in lace. For birthday parties I pressed my fingers onto my eyelids, painting them with denim-blue powder, and swept red ChapStick across my lips. I felt like a glamorous Pocahontas, a high-heeled Esmeralda, my olive skin and dark hair trimmed neatly around my green eyes. I was brave, I was loud, I loved hearing my tiny voice make shapes out of sound. I had big ideas for the world, and for myself.

I considered myself a princess, but at first not like Cinderella or Sleeping Beauty, although I *loved* their poofy gowns and hairstyles. I imagined myself more as Guinevere, fierce in the forest with her gladiator sandals and her bow, or as Morgan Le Fay, one day owning my own magical tree house full of books. I shared a birthday with Joan of Arc, which, to me, meant we shared more than just a birthday, but some kind of deeper moral quality, something only superheroes like her (. . . and me) had. I too believed I had the ability to bring an entire army to its knees.

But I wasn't supposed to be a hero, at least according to what was being consistently reinforced to me; I was just supposed to be a princess. My dad was always telling me to shut up and stop talking so much, to keep my ideas to myself.

I'm a daughter of Latine[2] immigrants, and in our culture, femininity for girls is so heavily enforced that my ears were pierced when I was three weeks old, tiny diamonds glittering in my tiny lobes. Girlhood was—literally—marked into me.

At six, my mom dressed me in vintage-style children's dresses, linen with farm animals hand-crocheted onto pockets. I wore headbands with giant bows, shining patent leather shoes, and always carried a tiny purse, just big enough to put my ChapStick in.

I wasn't taught to ask for what I wanted, or how to refuse what I didn't. No one ever showed me how to say no. I was taught to sit still, be pretty, and be an object a man would want to marry one day.

Depending on when you grew up, this may seem outrageous or totally relatable. The world looks a little different today. But it changed in my lifetime, and no matter how "woke" (bleh) society has become, that conditioning still runs deep in our veins and our culture.

---

2   Gender-neutral form of "Latino/a."

Throughout my childhood, because I was seen as, well, a girl, I couldn't do anything that was outside the bubble of ballet and piano lessons until my brother was old enough to do it too—even though I was the oldest. I couldn't have a sleepover, go to a concert, learn the guitar, ride a skateboard, see a PG-13 movie, or ride a bike until *he* was ready to do it too.

My brother, David, with his golden skin and glittering green eyes, was always pushing the limits of gravity. He'd do shit like hook up a skateboard to a car to see how fast he could skate, surf on the wake left behind by boats, jump out of helicopters to snowboard down virgin trails. He was forever getting himself into major injuries from his adventures, but nothing, and no one, ever stopped him.

He was raised to engage, wrestle with, and impose on the outside world around him. He was applauded. He was praised.

He was also incredibly sensitive, my brother, his softness always an invitation for closeness. As a boy, David was shy and introverted, peeking out from behind the legs of my mom in public, his wispy curls a curtain over his jade-colored eyes. My dad would yell at him because he had a hard time looking strangers in the eyes. As he grew up, he learned to hide the truer parts of himself, becoming a star athlete, a stud, the boy every girl and her mother across the ENTIRE Miami-Dade area wanted to date, and every boy wanted to be.

And yet, no one really knew him.

No one besides me, anyway.

He'd let me in every once in a while, crawling into bed with me as tears poured down his face after breakups in high school, just as he used to do when he was little, when our parents would be gone too long.

David's inner world was our little secret. It was sacred to me, and I kept it as safe as I could.

But while my brother was taught, and often forced, to exert himself on the world, as a young girl, I was taught to pull away from it.

I learned that girls were to be looked at, perceived, and that *this* was the only way to know ourselves—through the gaze of others. How we were received beneath that gaze was where we got the reward. I learned to be quiet, eventually. Learned to keep my ideas to myself, doing what I could to make myself disappear. But even so, I was bad at that too, apparently.

Instead of my eighth-grade yearbook being scrawled with "Love you, see you next year, don't ever change!" mine was covered in multiple iterations of scratchy middle-school boy handwriting spelling out "You're so hot."[3]

When I'd picked up the yearbook from my homeroom, my stomach had dropped as I flipped through the pages and landed on the school's "Most Attractive" superlative. There I was, smiling back at myself. It was a picture of me.

I was horrified and embarrassed. I had never wanted to stick out; I'd done everything I could to hide.

I hadn't *done* anything to earn this title except be looked at and witnessed in . . . doing nothing. Instead of this "prize" making me feel proud, it made me feel useless. It felt like the entire school had decided I wasn't good at anything else except

---

3   "For a Jewish girl, anyway."

the way I looked—which, yeah, I was bangin' for someone who was still really into Limited Too.

As I stepped into high school, this title gave boys, and even more painfully, girls, permission to mistreat, bully, and assault me—which was *not* the twist most might see coming from being such a tween hottie. It sucked, and it wasn't fun.

I realized then that no one really *knew* me, either.

We all kind of become big sacks of skin for gender to be projected onto us, a cinema script full of lines, costumes, and characters to play. We're taught to stay static, stay still, stay stagnant as the reel keeps shining its colors over us. No need to think or question, or even move—the film's already been made, and all we have to do is let it play.

But movies aren't real, and if we're expected to live like the filled-in outlines of actors on a screen, we wind up neglecting some pretty important pieces of being human in a body that functions.

For example, girls in movies don't poop, or get periods. And yet girls (and some nonbinary folks, and even a few boys!) in real life do.

The first time I got my period I thought I had shit myself in reverse, chunky brown stains suddenly all over my underwear.

I sat on the toilet staring at the skid marks, trying to figure out how my vagina could have secreted poop. What was happening to me?

I was twelve, alone in the school locker room bathrooms, where the toilet doors had too much space between them, and anyone walking past could peek inside. My stomach squirmed, and I realized I was about to shit myself *even more* from the stress that someone might walk in at any moment, discovering that me, a full-grown middle schooler, had just pooped her pants without even realizing it. Staring at the lumpy brown texture in my panties, I was disgusted with myself, trying to scrub out the goop with toilet paper, rolling a big wad of it between my legs before I lifted my underwear back up. I hobbled around the rest of the day, praying no one could smell me.

How depressing.

Sure, my parents never explicitly said that my body was *bad*, or that I was. They never verbalized specific rules around dating or desire. My dad loved the beauty of a woman's body.

But it became obvious that this appreciation did not apply to me.

My father laughed at my body loudly, like it was the funniest joke, pointing to my belly peeking out from a T-shirt, or the low-rise jeans that couldn't stretch fully around my hips, but then refused to let anyone else admire it. I couldn't go to parties or be picked up at home for a date. Papi wanted me always covered, away from men. Meanwhile, my mother always wore her breasts out, nipples hard and visible against any shirt she wore, telling me sex was something beautiful (!) but she didn't want me using tampons. I shouldn't lose my virginity to a cotton stick.

My whole upbringing was laced with mixed messages and shame.

This shame followed and crawled behind me like a shadow, casting itself over every experience that was meant to be pleasurable and only mine. Over time, I distanced myself further and further from the things I wanted, especially anything that had to do with sex.

My experience isn't unique. Many of us raised as girls have our own versions of shame-filled masturbation stories, terrible early sexual experiences, and reinforcement from the world around us that we are wrong for wanting literally anything at all.

I waited a lot longer than most people to have penetrative sex. It took me a long time to do it because I'd never really wanted to. Once I entered my twenties I felt like I couldn't make the excuse of "not being ready" anymore. I was the last one left to do it out of everyone I knew, so I did.

But it turned out sex was *not* the life-changing experience I'd been promised by . . . literally everyone. I could hardly even consider it tolerable. What was *soooo* great about being pounded into, eardrums ringing from the too-loud music bumping from the stereo system that took over half his room? What was so delicious about being instructed to stuff his dick into my mouth, holding my breath as I mentally calculated how I could get rid of the goopy yellow-white semen that was sticking all over the insides of my mouth without having to swallow it, *and* not offend him?

Even the memory makes me shudder, a bubble of nauseated spit caught in my throat.

It was my first year of college. The guy I was seeing was used to a lot of one-night stands. He was a drummer, a once-aspiring pro skater, and medical student. Hot shit. And while he was studying medicine at one of the fanciest universities, it was obvious he still did not know that I, too, could have an orgasm. How convenient. For him.

I hadn't had much sex, but I *had* read enough feminist theory by that point in my life to know that I was allowed—entitled, even—to my own pleasure. However, I never came. He came *Every. Single. Time.* Every single time!!! He'd whine and moan and *hurt*—"Arieeeelle, it *hurts!*"—if he didn't release. One chilly Tuesday afternoon after class, as the sun was setting and he was catching his breath from his third orgasm of the session, I kneeled down in front of him, folding my hands in my lap.

"Um, so you know that I'd like to come too, right? Like, maybe you could try going down on me."

His eyebrows furrowed as he looked down at the floor. When he looked back up at me again, his eyes were filled with such hurt and dismay that I understood I was the first woman to ever question his sexual abilities.

"Are you serious right now?" Mmm. He was defensive. "Go find someone else to fuck, then."

He stormed out of the room and I felt kind of bad that I'd hurt his feelings. Intellectually, I could point to all the ways in which it wasn't my job to please him, but my entire body screamed that it *absolutely* was. He came back into the room eventually but he refused to go down on me. That day, or ever.

Young me excused him, understood he wouldn't change overnight, or maybe ever. I didn't even like sex, so I guessed I couldn't really make a case for breaking up with him over unequal orgasms. We'd been seeing each other for a little while when one morning I woke up in his tiny twin bed, gray jersey sheets mirroring the snow falling out the dirty window, and felt my stomach cramp. I gasped, clutching myself, and felt him stir next to me. I slipped out of the covers quietly, praying he wouldn't wake up so I could take a shit in his shared bathroom without the pressure of him hearing me—I'd *never* be able to shit if he could hear me. Once out from under the covers, I turned back to the bed to pull the sheets back up, and I was mortified to see a rust-colored stain right where I had been, the same color that had covered my underwear all those years ago in the locker room bathroom.

I didn't have to shit—I had my period.

My period doesn't trickle in, it rages. I've been thinking about giving it a name, but nothing except "MY FUCKING PERIOD" feels right. It's a monster, this thing. It quite literally feels like I am being possessed. Every month since the very first one, the walls of my uterus are torn down and the blood of an entire population pours out of me. Every month, I am possessed by this FUCKING PERIOD. Every month, I am swept under the pull of my hormones, turning me into a bloated, angry, sensitive, howling, and hairy monster. Yes, even my chin hairs decide to sprout during this time.

Every month, all I have to do is stand and a fully produced immersive experience takes place between my legs, thick red rivers rolling down my thighs, spots sprouting all over the floor. My favorite is when I look into the toilet. Ribbons twirl in the water, spinning and swimming until they slowly sink to the bottom, a small hibiscus-colored pool. MY FUCKING PERIOD is painful and completely overpowering, but definitely a brilliant performance artist.

I used to think everyone who had periods had periods like me.

Pain so severe I see fireworks, eyes flickering, ready to pass out. Depressive episodes so deep that I forget half of the month I'm not like this—crying, overwhelmed, and worried that I'm too unstable to participate in society. Paralyzed and scared, I just as quickly become a creature with anger crackling her cells, ready to burn down anything that dares disturb her.

My breasts, already monstrous, become demons, nipples now blood-searching eyes. I can't take two steps without holding myself. I can't wear a bra or I cry.

I sleep with multiple pads and two towels—a bespoke blood-proofing suit that deserves a patent—and even with twenty-seven diapers attached to the lower half of my body (only a small exaggeration), I've still stained countless sheets just by accidentally rolling onto my side during the night.

Doctors don't know what to tell me. Everything looks normal, they say. You must just be extra sensitive to fluctuations in hormone levels. Nothing to be done, they say.

So it stays my problem. Me and my own allergic reaction to myself.

Back to bleeding on my college boyfriend's gross-ass bed—
Stepping back in horror from the stain of this menstrual "crime," I grabbed the coat I'd left on the floor the night before

and tiptoed out, completely embarrassed. I did an entire gymnastics routine in my head, trying to think of all the ways I could excuse the blood, ways in which he might not even notice it.

It'd be at least a week until I saw him again anyway. With MY FUCKING PERIOD, it'd be impossible for me to have sex. I assumed there'd be no point in seeing him until I was "better." Back then, I *truly* believed that there wasn't a reason for this guy to spend time with me when he couldn't have sex with me. I skulked back to my place in the windy snow, holding my jacket tight against my chin. I stepped into my warm, wood-floored, stained-glass-windowed home, grateful to be back in my own— clean—space. I changed my underwear and climbed into my own bed. I could be calm now, wrapped in the safety of my house filled with friends who loved every bloody piece of me.

The next day I ran into him as I was walking to class, his face growing pale as he saw me.

"Yesterday after you left, I saw blood in my bed." His eyes were wide, pupils severe, poking into mine.

I looked back at him blankly, with a feigned compassion. "Oh no," I said, my stomach sinking. I'd been caught.

"I totally freaked out."

"Of course you did." I remained externally calm, placing a hand on his arm. "Did you figure out what it was?" I asked innocently.

"Well, I thought it was your period blood—like, *so* disgusting." He scrunched his nose and stuck out his tongue for that last part.

I instinctively recoiled, burning with shame.

He started laughing. "But it wasn't! I was fuckin' bugging *out*, but then I saw I had a cut on my toe. It was just my toe blood, so it was all good." He smiled at me, reached for my hand.

I froze.

Just toe blood?

All of a sudden, FEMINISM snapped into clarity for me.

Toe blood was something that sounded gross. Blood, coming from a college boy's toe. Yeah, disgusting. We can all agree. So how was blood from *his* crusty-ass toe somehow *less* disgusting than my monthly menstruation? He seemed to have no problem putting his dick where that blood came out any chance he got. Suddenly, for him to be so disturbed by my body made him pathetic to me. I felt the burn of my previous shame turn into a different kind of heat—anger.

I realized he *was* pathetic. And so was I for feeling bad about the perfectly natural and normal organic function that happens in a healthy body, the body that he insisted on controlling (*that dress is too short, suck my dick, come over*) in the name of some faraway, yet acutely immediate, desire.

So I kept it a secret. It was *my* blood, after all.

I broke up with the misogynistic medicine-studying musician at my graduation. We had talked about it for weeks; he knew it was coming. But he smoked a lot of weed. Like, so much weed that he forgot our entire breakup. Months later, he was texting me, angry that I wasn't letting him visit when he was in my city. What kind of girlfriend was I?

I'm not your girlfriend, I messaged. *We're broken up.*

What are you talking about? Yes you are.

I rolled my eyes.

No, we're not.

I'm in town. I want to see you.

He texted me again. *You can't deny me that.*

I felt guilty, like I was hurting him. So I said fine. He could come visit.

I let him upstairs to my new grown-up apartment, showing him the art I'd hung up on the walls myself. It was only a little while before he started forcing me, as I sobbed, and eventually obliged, tears falling from my face forming a shaking puddle on his body.

I stopped getting my periods for years after that.

It's kind of beautiful, how much our bodies know what our minds don't yet. We hold all those feelings, first as wounds, then as armor.

For so much of my life, I carried the shame of my body, and it only made me suffer. It made me shrink, be quiet, and cross my legs. It made me do things with my body I didn't want to, shave off pieces of my body I didn't want to, starve and contort my body in ways I didn't want to. It made me perform "pretty" and pretend that my period and my poop didn't exist.

But all that shame wasn't mine. It never had been. It was always everyone else's.

It was my mother's, who used to admonish me for leaving pads out in my room where my brother could see.

It was my brother's, who'd get mad at me for peeing with the bathroom door slightly open, infuriated that he was forced to know that I had bodily functions just like he did.

It was my father's, who never spoke to me about my body at all, except to make fun of it or control how I used it.

It was only years later, when I finally got my period back, that I started appreciating having one. MY FUCKING PERIOD is dramatic, but it's actually pretty cool. Having a period told me my body was working exactly as it should. So what had made me believe there was something broken with me to begin with?

When had I learned my blood ➤ therefore my body ➤ therefore my existence ➤ was bad?

Well, from everywhere. From school, which separated us by gender when it was time to learn about periods, granting boys permission to never have to learn about what happened to our bodies, the same bodies they would continue having opinions about, forcing themselves on, and making up laws around.

From the reactions that boys (and teachers!) had given girls in middle school, when we spotted without knowing, our khaki shorts dotted with a little brown stain.

From all the TV shows I watched as a kid, and later as an adult, that never once showed people talking about periods, let alone having them, as if this very real, monthly experience were something not even worth mentioning or writing into a script.

From my religion, which told me I required a cleansing and didn't allow some imaginary future husband to touch me for two weeks (or more!) until I was "clean" again, sure to not carry a single drop of blood.

From the yoga studios I went to, which advised no participation for the first three days of a period and technically didn't allow for a male teacher to touch me during that time.

And from the menstruation industry itself, which reinforces the shame over and over through names like "Aunt Flo" and "red visitor," euphemisms like "feminine care aisle"—which, ew—and commercials featuring blue liquid sprinkled on pads (*very* unlike the thick, gloppy, stringy soup of viscous red material that comes out of me each month).

What an easy way to make us shrink, to belittle our bodies, our brains.

If you've ever dared to ask yourself who you really are and what you actually like, that's a bravery and a defiance against *centuries* of shame stories that you, and all your ancestors, have spent whole lives existing in.

Those shame stories used to be a way to keep us safe, but a lot of those protective instincts aren't working out great for us anymore. A lot of these instincts are actually *keeping* us from living a life that's fully alive.

They stop us from accessing ourselves and stop us from intimately connecting with others. Goddess forbid they see through all the things we're trying so hard to hide! It's a privilege to bend gender expression and move beyond being a "good girl," certainly, but it's also true that there's a lot more space today for expansion and variation from previously held definitions. There's a lot more space for anyone to deviate from what's considered "acceptable," and although it's still a massively fucked-up world, it's not gonna get better, and it'll certainly never change, unless each of us changes first.

If you're terrified of confronting your *own* self, you're not going to have much space for someone else to be themselves either.

As overwhelming as it all may or may not seem, it's pretty cool to even *have* the awareness that any of this shame stuff is going on inside us, because once we can name it, it no longer has to define us. We each get to choose the labels, expressions, and experiences we want for ourselves.

We get to reject or change the definitions of the words we call ourselves.

Everything we are now gets to be good and beautiful and right.

Good girls don't exist, but we do.

We get to name our deviations as glorious.

We get to kneel at the altar of our own voice.

We get to dress ourselves in capes, miniskirts, or well-tailored suits.

We get to buzz our hair or let it grow long.

We get to inject hormones, get top surgery, or buy some boobs.

We each get to write our own story from the ground up, start over, and reclaim it all.

To say it simply: What if being bad wasn't just okay, but the only way to be *good* to ourselves?

What if being bad actually just means coming home to yourself? Stripping off the costume you wear for the world and stepping into the clothes that feel just right?

Because if being a Bad Girl means taking all the scary steps toward myself, regardless of what anyone else thinks, then yes, please, sign me up.

That's not to say that when society, our parents, or anyone else tells us we're bad, it doesn't feel horrible. It can make us feel worthless, shameful, good for nothing, and small. Even as a self-proclaimed Bad Girl, I still have to make space for all the feelings that come up when I feel rejected because of who I am.

But, ultimately, being *down* with being Bad actually feels . . . fucking awesome. It feels like freedom, like magic, like I am exactly who I'm meant to be. It's not always easy, and it can feel lonely, but then, all of a sudden, I don't feel lonely anymore. Because all of a sudden, I've gotten much closer to *me*.

Today, my dog's favorite time of the month is my period. My bloated pads are his favorite treat. He sneaks into the bathroom, sniffs through the garbage, and somehow I always find him on the carpet, happily lying next to and protecting his bloody prize.

At first I thought I should be grossed out, embarrassed, ashamed. Pads soaked in blood appearing all over the house? No!

But actually, every time I find him hiding with his stolen goods, I laugh with pride. This creature who loves me also loves MY FUCKING PERIOD. He doesn't shame me; he doesn't tell me it's wrong. He loves what my body does, and he reminds me that I have every reason to love it too.

He's an animal, as am I.

Today, I always reach for my pubes as I think. I never wear pants if I can help it, and long, dark hairs curl out from behind the seams of my underwear, a thin nest cushioning each side of my thighs.

My fingers are forever drawn to the texture, a meditation of silk and softness. I stroke the sides and often slip my hands beneath my waistband, twirling the hairs around like a spool. My thighs look like the vine-colored walls around my house, roots, leaves, flowers sprouting all over in abundance. They slip out when I wear shorts that are really short, and they announce themselves loudly when I'm in a bikini thong. Sometimes I try to squeeze my legs together so no one can see, and other times I proudly pull the thong straps even higher and let everyone enjoy the view.

It's still a complicated relationship, my hair, my blood, my body, and I.

But the beginning is just that: a first step.

It's not about undoing all you've become, because, first of all, who you are is beautiful and expansive and whole as is. You're reading this book—you are already a *bad*ass[4]—and anyway, we *can't* undo all we've become, at least gender-wise.

This stuff's been injected into us in utero, and to have any kind of expectation that we'll somehow rid ourselves of it completely isn't helpful. Better to have fun with it.

---

4   Unbiased opinion.

Better to flip our relationship to gender from suffocation to play.

Think back to the first time you were told you were being "bad," the first time you felt like something was just *wrong* with you, whether it was the way you ate, the way you dressed, or the way you talked. The first time you were rejected. The first time you disappointed someone.

Whatever it was, it can probably be traced back to your gender—and how you expressed it.

By embracing the "bad," we can start releasing all the shame we've carried and actually find out who we are, with love, curiosity, and acceptance.

So let's figure this out together.

Step 1: Define the bad.

Get out a notebook if you want, or open up an empty doc on your computer. What does it *mean* to be bad?

Start a list of all the ways you've felt like you've been bad.

For example:

Ways I've felt like I've been bad: eating too much dessert, wearing dresses that are too tight, and my weight fluctuations.

Reflect on the feelings that have come up throughout your life when you've been "bad." What are your feelings around those parts of yourself now?

Step 2: Explore where we learned this shit from.

Where did you learn that those parts of you were "bad"? Whose voice is in your head telling you they are? Is it society, your parents, a teacher? Were those lessons implied or explicitly told? How were they reinforced?

For example:

Who told me this was bad? I learned that having a certain type of body takes "control," and because I didn't have that body, society, my parents, and '90s media told me it was my fault—both directly and indirectly through whom they reinforced as role models. I was taught that only those who were lazy gained weight, and only those who were slutty had boobs.

Step 3: Time to reframe.

What if all the things we've been told are bad actually *aren't*? Not at all.

The hierarchy of being human is made up. There is no "good" or "bad"—there's just human. Being human is a *beautiful* thing, and choosing to do it in the ways that uniquely express our bodies and minds is something kinda like art.

So in your notebook or document, next to your list of "bad," see if you can reframe all the "bad" bits.

For example:

The bad: I have felt like a bad girl when I have worn clothes that showed too much cleavage or too much skin because I was taught by my father, and then reinforced through society, that this made me stupid, dirty, and immoral—not just for showing it, but also for having a body like mine in the first place.

Reframe: Wearing shirts with cleavage has no moral factor. The shape of my body has no moral factor. Wearing what I want on my body is an act of power, self-expression, and self-love. It's a GOOD thing to be confident in my body and express agency over it. This does not make me bad!!!!

Step 4: Embrace it. Let's be Bad.

Here is THE kick: The only way to be yourself is to be "bad," in some way or another, according to society.

So fuck it, let's be Bad.

Let's be Bad and ourselves. Let's be Bad and full of joy. Let's be Bad and live the lives we want, the way we want, how we want. Let's shed all the shit that's been forced on us throughout our lifetimes and break out of the boxes filled with shame. Let's find those pieces of ourselves we've felt afraid of and let them see the light, let them shine, let them live.

DAUGHTER

"If the wounds are ancestral, the medicine must be ancestral as well."

—*Dr. Jennifer Mullan*

I remember the day I walked down the stairs and accidentally grazed my chest against the curving wall, rounding the corner. It felt like a bird's beak had plunged itself into my skin, its feathers fluttering as the bruise blossomed across my nipple. I thought something was wrong, maybe I was dying—and a part of me was. I was entering puberty.

Papi pulled me aside. I must have been twelve years old.

"You don't have your mother's genes." He meant her curveless body, her six-pack, leg muscles like a ballerina. "You have mine. The women in my family . . ." He trailed off, looking around the room for inspiration. "They get *wide*." He said this with a curt nod of his head, clearly proud of his word choice. He looked at me seriously. "You have to be careful."

It was a warning.

On the outside, my childhood was a fantasy, a vision of foreign dreams coming true.

I grew up with Biscayne Bay as my backyard, the clear water turning a deep blue the farther out I looked. The land behind my room was dotted in palm and banyan trees, their big leaves moving seductively with the wind. I spent tropical weekends playing with my brother in the mud when it rained, making makeshift contraptions out of whatever we could find in order to get as high as possible before jumping into our limestone-framed pool. Boats of all sizes would slip by our house, our own yacht tied up to the dock, blasting the kind of Cuban salsa my dad loved to dance to, in a city filled with everyone holding on to the pieces of home they'd left behind. It was a magical time to be living in Miami, a place where few had been born and everyone had fought to arrive.

The whirlwind story of my parents' meeting went something like this: My father, at a singles JCC[5] picnic—gefilte fish[6] and bourekas[7] sharing space on the wooden table, Michael Jackson blaring out the boombox—adjusted his oversized glasses to better lay eyes on my mother, eighteen years old and upside down, walking on her hands in the grass.

---

5   Jewish Community Center: Think Jewish basketball leagues and social events.
6   Salty fish cakes, a delicacy of Ashkenazi Jews, but not particularly appetizing if you ask me.
7   Phyllo pastry stuffed with cheese and other flavorings, a *much* better delicacy of Sephardi Jews. The matriarchs at my synagogue have refused to share the recipe for decades—"the young ones will steal it and sell their own, *then* how will we raise money for the temple?"—even though they're all so old we're worried they'll die before anyone else learns how to make them.

"Who's *that*?" my dad asked his friend, without taking his eyes off her.

He didn't have to point her out. His friend already knew whom he was talking about.

"Her name's Masha. Just got here from Guatemala last month."

My dad kept staring.

"I'm going to marry her," he said. And he did.

A few years later, they had me.

The expectations that had been placed on me to be a good girl had come from the world around me—the specific socio-cultural moment I was born into. "Good girl" was collective and singular. Depending on when you were born and where, similar expectations may have been placed on you and everyone else around you. For me, at the time of my birth in Miami, there really was only *one* way to be a good girl—and anything outside of that was bad.

A good daughter, on the other hand . . .

Those expectations are handed down through the generations of our own very specific familial lineages, becoming polished in the process, a truck full of stones dragging behind our ancestors, ready to be offloaded onto our bodies the moment we're born. Of course, as daughters, we're affected by the rules around being a "good girl" in society, but even as times have changed and feminism has flourished, for some of us, little has changed inside the fences of our families.

Every single one of us is a child of someone else. Our family dynamics and expectations do not exist in a vacuum, and the reclamation of our experiences has to begin with mapping out the constellation of the expectations unique to our own family, our own lineage, every piece we each inherited without even realizing it.

None of us has remained unscathed in the handing down of familial bullshit.

Here's what was passed down to me:

A good daughter was supposed to be a doll Mami could dress up, her purpose to wake up in the morning. I was supposed to need her and look up to her, not be more independent than she was. Her entire life she'd had a mother who always put her down and made her feel useless. And now *she* was the mother, doing the same thing without even meaning to.

A good daughter was supposed to be a legacy Papi could leave behind, a prize won of the hardship his family had lived through, a stoic creature who could survive revolutions and stay silent unless spoken to. Like Mami, Papi was also resentful of me, but in an entirely different way. As a kid, I understood that he loved me, but it was also clear he saw me as an impediment to his relationship with his wife. He worked too much, and the time he had with my mother was sacred. So his solution was to "toughen me up"; that way I wouldn't need her so much.

To my mother, I was a know-it-all, superficial, too tough. And to my father, I was overly sensitive, an idealist, weak with empathy.

I felt in constant whiplash with myself. How could I be both too tough and too weak? Too hard and too soft? Since the moment I was born, I seemed to be doing it wrong.

It meaning being their daughter.

I didn't understand it as a child, but the expectations my parents had of me weren't theirs alone. They'd been passed down through generations, molded and shaped through lived experience. My father believed in discipline, in rule following, in little soldiers who bowed to his every command. My mother, in rebellion against her own upbringing, believed in freedom, in no clothes and no rules, in endless space to discover who these children would become (as long as they became something she understood, something that was like her). They both earnestly believed in their ideals, believed in their styles of parenting, believed they were doing it "right."

I certainly don't have all the answers, but I do know their styles of parenting—taken individually, and together—fucked me up.

I always think back to these words Dr. Jennifer Mullan wrote and posted in 2022: "Gentle reminder that healing generational trauma is not a goal. It is a beautiful by-product of living a life of true expression & acknowledging your ancestral experiences, while unlearning your internalized programming. You are magnificent. Glow & your lineage will too."[8]

We don't need to change to live a fulfilling life—all we need to do is glow as we already are! The idea that we need to be "better" or "heal" is colonized thought disguising itself. The idea

---

8   Mullan, J. [@decolonizingtherapy]. (2023, January 24). *Gentle reminder that healing generational trauma is not a goal. It is a beautiful by-product of living a life of* [Digital graphic]. Instagram. https://www.instagram.com/p/Cnz_CJtPVm1

that you are not enough, exactly as you are, is white supremacy. There is no goal or outcome for life; there's just living it. No one wins a prize for enlightenment, for breaking patterns, for doing things differently than their parents did. The whole experience, and the wisdom and peace you might gain from it, is the point.

We might all have different starting points, but we are all composed of intergenerational experiences. Our genetic makeup is composed of millions of cells, each shaped and birthed through our ancestors. This is how we came to be. This is how we were made.

But this is your body, no one else's. This is your experience, and how you relate to the land, the people, and the skies around you is a choice you get to make.

I've got so much of the world in my blood I don't even know what, or who, is all there.

"You know, according to some people, you're technically not even fully Jewish."[9]

This is something my abuela only ever tells me when she's upset at me because it's the most pointed insult she could ever throw.

But when I ask about my ancestors, all the different countries and languages they come from, she stares at me unblinking with her pool-green eyes, purple sparkle eyeshadow

---

9   Judaism is matrilineal, but my mother's mother converted. According to Abuela #1, Abuela #2's conversion was not as "kosher" as she would have liked. But Abuela #2 converted in a time when six million Jews had all just been gassed to death, so the Holy Rabbis were down to accept whoever they could get.

shimmering over the Shabbat table as her matching purple kaftan drapes to the floor. "Ariellita, I don't understand these questions. What does it matter where anyone's from? They're Jewish. You're Jewish. That's all that matters."[10]

My connection to my Hebrew indigeneity mattered, but it was never *all* that mattered to me because my family wasn't Jewish like other people's families were Jewish. My family was dark-skinned and spiced, our holiday food a mixture of arroz con pollo, platanos, kibbeh, and dolmas. My family wasn't liberal like the Ashkenazi Jews around us or the few I saw on TV; my family remained confused about how a woman could be a rabbi and hid all the queerness from our blood. Other Jewish parents took their kids to protests, bought them books on feminism, had guitars playing during services. Not mine.

My family practices Sephardic traditions, but we're actually ethnically Romaniote.[11] Turkish blood is our most recent ancestry, but so is Polish, Portuguese, Mongolian, Indigenous Mayan, and probably Moroccan too. I'm a child of immigrants from Cuba and Guatemala—political refugees whose parents and grandparents were also political refugees. Such is the story of the Jewish Diaspora, especially if where they've landed keeps getting destabilized by politicians after sugarcane, bananas, and Indigenous blood.

When I was a child, my mom would tuck me into bed, put her hands over my eyes, and sing me the Shema. She'd always

---

10   Some bits of this are from a piece I wrote for *Hey Alma* in 2023, "I'm Jewish. But I'm Also Latina."

11   A tiny and nearly erased sect of Jews with Middle Eastern ancestry coming out of Greece (there's barely any of us left), and one of the oldest Jewish communities in the world!

end with "*que Dios te bendiga y te proteja*,"[12] the prayer of the mothers in Guatemala, a primarily Catholic country.

I have so many ancestors, I don't have the space to weave the threads of their stories here. Some, like my abuelo's, made it into a multipage spread in *LIFE* magazine, while others, like his brother, ended in a Mexican prison (after a successful underground tunnel escape!).[13] My mom's brother died of AIDS during her pregnancy with me, and her father died from war shrapnel that impaled his ribs. There were many others who died in gas chambers during the Holocaust, and everyone else . . . well, they went from country to country seeking refuge and a new home.

Thus begins the context for my story, the foundations already laid out before I ever arrived. Their hopes, dreams, and traumas already seeping into the cells that would form my belly, my ears, my lips, and my toes. The world and values my great-grandparents passed down to their children, then to their children, then to me.

I was the pride and joy of my family . . . for the first year and a half of my life.

My mom was terrified of another miscarriage like she'd had the year before me, and she cared for me with everything she had while I was in her body, and once I pushed myself out of it.

---

12   "May G-d bless you and protect you."
13   BIG story for another time.

I was born with a little raspberry mark that she'd make sure to sun every day in the soft morning light, trying to make what she thought was a "rash" go away. I'd be on my belly naked, no diapers, my tiny butt positioned toward the windows. She knew exactly how to be there for me, knew what to give me, knew what I was needing when I cried.

I was an extension of her, made by her and of her.

But once I learned to move and steer my own body, to put food into my mouth and use words to communicate, something changed. She grew resentful of me.

Before I even had solid memories, I was already letting her down.

To Mami, somehow, my individuation made me ungrateful and difficult. I didn't need her like I used to, didn't want her like I used to. And more than anything, I wasn't *her*. She was beautiful, but I looked nothing like her. I was a better reader at five than she'd ever been, and I had no problem digging my little feet into the ground and telling her so. I was good at school, while she didn't get the chance to graduate. I may not have been as beautiful as she was, but I was smart, and I held on to that as my power. Even at this age, my father had already taught me that insecurity and weakness were things to be repulsed by, and I could always sniff them on her. Her anger boiled right underneath her skin. So did mine.

Thanks to my abuelo's legacy in the shoe business and "making it in America," Papi was able to go and make his own American Dreams come true. Several businesses later across quite a few industries, he values hard work, discipline, and speaking up. He's beautiful, with slick dark hair and dark skin, an easy smile that often makes him mistaken for a celebrity.

The only person who outshines him is my mother, with her long blond hair and tall, tight body. She has a feminine and otherworldly energy that has always served as a perfect foil to Papi's ultra-masculinity (even while he wears salmon-colored pants and purple suits, swearing by the boutiques he shops at in South Florida, all catering to gay men, which he shares with glee). My whole life everyone has always said Mami is not of this earth, even when her children desperately needed her to be.

Me and my brother, David, who was only a year and a half younger than me and raised as my twin, were forever caught in the tides of our parents' yin and yang energies, until their opposite forces turned from magnetic to repellent, and they divorced—shattering the glassy illusion of this picture-perfect family.

But before that, there we were: a (literal) model for a mother, a successful businessman as a father—the model minority family.

My brother and I were beautiful—immaculately dressed, exceptionally educated, perfectly assimilated to the country my parents both escaped to.

We spent winters at our house in the mountains, aspen trees glittering their leaves goodnight. We spent summers sailing the Caribbean, watching my little sister learn to walk on white sugar sand. Mornings before school I'd look out my window, the one that looked straight into the sea, and run outside in my underwear, checking the weather with the breeze.

This was the happy ending of a generational history of struggle, displacement, suffering, and resilience.

This was the story of hard work and perseverance paying off. This was the story of traditional values, dreaming big enough, and sacrificing what one needed to in order to make it all come true.

But there's always more to a story.

It's so easy to look at someone's else's life on the outside and believe we're seeing it all, but that's never true. Most of us have been taught to keep all our suffering hidden.

Nobody[14] had any clue about all the shit that was happening within the walls of my family, and it was outright expected of us that we keep it that way.

What everyone saw on the outside was the shiny surface of a tangled mess of control, shaming, pressure, and trauma.

I was raised in a way to assimilate as much as possible to this country, to those who held power, to whiteness,[15] to wealth. My identities weren't something to linger on, to hold on to, to explore. On the surface it seemed like I was having the experience of the wealthy white kids around me, but in reality, my story is the story of refugees, of a family that has had to escape

---

14   NOBODY!
15   Papi and my tío—both VISIBLY and very brown—have spent their whole lives considering themselves white, even while never being treated that way by society. I imagine it was always easier to blame themselves for how they were treated, because they could change, than blame what they looked like and where they were from, which they couldn't.

to a new country, a new culture, and a new world every generation.

Pressure, expectation, ambition—these were the things that have kept my family safe for generations, so they were forced even more on us. I was to never forget that "you've been given everything."[16]

Papi worked hard to give me a life that would be easier than his, and his father's. But without realizing it, he was instilling what every father before him had instilled in him: that there was a certain kind of trade for the suffering of our ancestors. Being given everything a child could need or want, I knew nothing of the world, according to him—not even my own self. So he controlled me.

"Everything comes with a price." He taught me that.

My father's always been a man who stops a room the moment he walks into it. He's a better orator than Obama and the most charismatic man on earth, when he chooses. His confidence, his clarity, his direction—these are all things I have because of him.

He inflates with attention, becomes his truest self in the spotlight—in many ways, just like me—but that's only if he's in the mood. Otherwise, he stays silent, simply watching, his mouth a flat line across his face.

Papi takes his coffee on the balcony and doesn't allow anyone near him until he's done. His physical space is spotless,

---

16   No presh, right?

partially because he's erected plastic gates around his things so that no children or dog can get past.[17] His favorite film is Snoop Dogg's *Soul Plane*, and he spent his twenties as a professional New York City ballet dancer, pink tights and all. The girls at my school all had crushes on him, and he got profiled as *Ocean Drive* magazine's Most Eligible Bachelor when I was a teen.[18]

Right around his divorce he became a cliche[19]—he bought a Porsche[20] and got into motorcycles. It was the second Monday of middle school when, at 11:59 a.m., a strange man in leathers pulled up in front of the cafeteria on a black Harley. On closer inspection, I realized it was my father.

"*What?*" He looked at me with the half smile he does when he knows he's gone too far. "I can't just join my daughter for lunch?"

And as smooth and charming as he's capable of being, making you feel like a million and one bucks, he also has the same capacity to diminish, belittle, and make you feel immediately, imminently worthless.

He routinely walks away from a conversation the minute he's no longer interested, leaving the other person talking to themselves. He has no patience, not much empathy, and simply hangs up when he's done with a phone call. He doesn't say anything, just hangs up.

He's modeled a life without people-pleasing or caring what other people think, except that instead of these qualities being

---

17   True fact.
18   The man's pushing seventy and women OF ALL AGES still come up to him all the time to try their luck.
19   As many recently divorced middle-aged men do.
20   Which he couldn't drive unless he put in his back cushion support.

passed down to me, I just trailed behind him, smoothing over everyone he pissed off along the way. But in the end, there were few, because he'd so easily and instantly make you fall in love with him again the moment he put his attention back on you.

The outside world knows Papi as the first person on the invite list to a party, but it was always very different at home.

After all, he was the father. Just like his father was, and his father before him. He always made sure to call this out. He was not our friend, and never would be.

Papi did not coddle. He was extremely frugal with praise. His parenting philosophy was that of the Russian ballet teachers he'd studied under in his twenties—breath was only to be used on those who had potential, and that breath would never be wasted on such a useless thing as a compliment. Use it for criticism, for improvement, for development instead.

He did not believe in emotions or disabilities—these were weaknesses to simply overcome—you wouldn't survive revolutions, hunger, and displacement if you were "sensitive." I was constantly reminded that my very nature was an inconvenience at the best of times and a disgusting disappointment at the worst.

"Don't you dare start with that shit." My father closed in on my face and bore into my seven-year-old eyes. "*Snap*," his lips disappeared, "*out of it*." I could see his teeth.

It worked. I stopped stuttering.

Papi treated his children like some people treat their dogs. "*No!*" he'd yell with such a boom that I could feel the reverb like a bomb detonating in my chest. "*Sit!*" spit sprinkling out of his mouth as he snapped it.

We never went out to dinner without being told the price. My brother and I learned to never ask for anything—not a present, not even a hug. It all had to be earned, and we should be grateful for what we got. If we got too close to him when he was busy, he'd yell "*Scram!*" his finger a deadly weapon pointing toward the door, and we'd run, our little hearts exploding with fear.

If we got too close to him when he wasn't busy, he'd look at us with his head tilted, a confused and frustrated expression on his face. "I don't understand." He'd raise his voice, hiccupping his question with mocking laughter. "Why can't you both just leave me alone? Why is that so hard for you? Leave. Me. *Alone*."

He could sniff out any weakness, which, as a daughter and son who were absolutely *desperate* for his affection, we had lots of, and he always made it clear it disgusted him.

We were terrified of him—as kids, but also for most of our adult life. It wasn't until recently I was able to teach my dad to not just say "Thanks" and hang up every time I told him I loved him on the phone, or to ask him to communicate nicely if I was near him and he wanted to be left alone.

A huge piece of my father's identity is father. He's had five children spanning across three different generations and has spent the majority of his life being a parent. As much as he's devoted to his role and invests heavily in all of us, he's never seemed to reflect on how his version of fatherhood has impacted us, and whether it actually *worked* for any of us. He's never seemed to consider that maybe all any of his kids needed was just to be accepted as we were. We didn't want to be coached, pushed, rejected, snapped out of it, or molded—we just wanted the chance to learn who we were and trust in that. Instead, we were taught that we should trust *him*, and never ourselves.[21]

Nowadays, there are far more fathers practicing gentle parenting, who are making space for their children to learn and grow and figure themselves out without judgment or desire for control. Papi has incorporated a lot of this into raising his two youngest.

I sometimes feel jealous of them, growing up with a dad who was nothing like mine. But it's a wonderful thing to witness the cultural ideas of parenthood shifting, and to see my dad shifting too—at least, with them. He's *still* pretty much the same way with me, and I'm *still* unraveling the lasting impacts of that . . . as you can tell.

Everything we experience informs everything else, and if our childhood was filled with feeling like we were "wrong" for just being ourselves and needing what we needed, it stays with us. Each of our personal stories and family histories differ, but we can all relate to the inevitable projection of expectations from our parents onto us. We've *all* been set up to fail, to feel like it was our fault. We're not the only ones—it happened to our parents and their parents too.

For me, I didn't yet realize that all of this was passed down. I didn't yet know that these weren't feelings for me to personally internalize, to take on, to make my own. Shit got dark. I

---

21   If any part of my experience resonates with you, I recommend reading *Adult Children of Emotionally Immature Parents* by Lindsay C. Gibson.

was not even ten years old when the darkness inside me compressed itself into something tangible, something that felt almost foundational. All of a sudden, this badness seemed to be, simply, me.

I *was* bad.

And *believing* I was bad was the final validation to everything I was already learning to believe about myself—that I was weak, I was undisciplined, and I needed too much. And since all of this was who I was—something I'd never be able to change—the only solution was to obliterate myself completely.

The badness controlled me, overwhelmed me, and dragged me by the hair through eating disorders, severe depression, and a lifetime of mental health crises. I also developed a secret. A very dark, very lonely secret that no one could ever find out—or surely I would be condemned forever.

I believed Papi would die if I turned off the faucet the wrong way. I would make Mami sick if I brushed my hair incorrectly. It was proof I was evil if I didn't close the door the right way, the way that felt *right*, the way that would save all of our lives. At least two hours of my day, every day, were spent repeating these compulsions—opening and closing the door dozens (and dozens) of times, switching the lights on and off repeatedly, ripping my hair out with my brush. And then, I started seeing penises everywhere, hairy vaginas haunting my mind. These were not sexy images. They were terrifying. It sounds ridiculous now, but back then, my world would randomly start closing in from giant penises, and I wanted to scream. And while wrinkled genitalia were plastered all over my mind's eye, every time I spoke, or had a single thought, I was writing the sentences forward and backward, forward and backward, sometimes spinning my body until I got dizzy, hoping it might make it stop (it didn't, it just made me have to spin equally the other direction too). All this, and I continued to mentally undress every single person I passed. I hated myself. This made it all worse. I had obsessive compulsive disorder so extreme that I was in a constant disassociation from my body, the world around me turning into a derealization nightmare of funhouse mirrors. The world was hazy, and I didn't feel alive. I became suicidally depressed at ten years old. I hovered over myself like a ghost, wearing my most beautiful dress and a big bow in my hair. I didn't exist. Yet I existed so much it was excruciating.

You couldn't really tell, though, unless you looked closely, which nobody did.

To the world, I was a high-achieving, high-functioning, high-performing child, never mind that the performance was literal. My entire life was pretend. I was always smiling, always grateful, always open. I didn't ask for anything, never demanded any space. To the world, I was a perfect daughter, then a perfect young woman. No one knew what was really happening, no one knew how cosmically alone I felt, no one knew *me*. But that was the point, because if no one knew me—the me that'd always been rejected, discarded, and ignored—perhaps I'd have a shot at being loved.

So, as long as I kept being "good," kept playing my role, kept performing, I could have control. I could keep everyone from finding out. I could have some semblance of power in the outside world that I seemed absolutely unable to have over myself.

But the thing with OCD is the more you try to control it, the more it controls you.

And all the while I was trying to obsessively control my insides, my parents were obsessively trying to control my outsides.

I had always been little, smooth skin covering a body that looked just like my brother's, but as my chest got fleshier, lumpy little mounds of fat poking through my T-shirts, my stomach ballooned outward, the hem of whatever I was wearing always riding up. I loved sweets (*"I don't have a sweet tooth—I have five!"*), and now my parents targeted that craving.

Mami didn't allow any refined sugar in the house. She didn't allow anything processed, or canned, or inorganic. Our pantry was a chemistry lab, glass jars filled with nuts, seeds, and grains I still don't know the names of. Our fridge was lined with the results of all her experiments—sprouted beet chips and cashew cookies (delicious), spirulina bread and flaxseed crackers (sandpaper on my tongue). Fig Newtons were the only poison allowed in the cupboards. I ate them like grapes.

I'd been learning to use my body to rebel against my parents' control, stuffing my face with food when no one else was home, hiding in the bathroom, eating the croissants and muffins only reserved for visiting guests, letting my belly fatten and balloon out, proof of my nightly binges. But when puberty hit, my body rebelled against me.

My body morphed beyond anything *anyone* could control. My breasts baked into brown muffins, their soft tops spilling out of any bra I put them into. They were full and alive, like the rest of me. My belly had flattened, and the shape of my body morphed into the kind of body "that's all over *Playboy* magazine, the kind of body people *pay* to have!" (said my mother, who had, in fact, paid). For fifteen years I wouldn't be able to walk outside without being stopped, called at, talked to, yelled at, leered at, and hissed at by men, sometimes up to three or four times on a block. I felt frozen, disgusted, shy, pleased. I had no idea how I was supposed to feel or respond. I did my best to hold my head high and keep walking, quietly blaming myself for going out in a dress, for running, for wearing a sweater, for existing at all.

Papi no longer laughed at my body. Now it was his turn to be angry.

I couldn't go to the movies, go to parties, go on dates. What I wore was scrutinized, put down, shamed.[22] How I existed was closely monitored—and I was way too afraid of him to rebel, so instead, I learned to police myself, doing everything I could to make myself even smaller than I already was.

The first time I ever felt the jolt of sexual desire, a tongue slipping against mine, I kept seeing my father in the distance mad at me, even though he wasn't actually there.

I had cast his own spell around myself, his image constantly watching, judging, weighing me. Ghost Daddy forever following me around.[23]

Even if he wasn't there, I felt he knew what was happening, that it would only take a moment before he'd appear out

---

22   Ha! It still is!
23   Absolutely NOT in a hot way.

of nowhere to see me as a woman, an individual, a body that deserved pleasure and freedom on its own. His love had always felt conditional, and I was terrified of disappointing him so deeply that he'd never want me close again.

I was always anxious, even as a child, crawling into bed with my parents every night when they were home. I'd slip out from my room, into their sheets, and between their bodies so that they might protect me from all the terrors that happened in my head.

Papi didn't like that I was messing up the marital bed, so he started locking me in my room every night.

I wailed by the door, fell asleep on the floor.

Mami sat on the other side of it, crying too.

My parents could not be more different—which is what had first attracted them to each other in the first place. Papi, the stable and stoic charmer. Mami, the free spirit who got along better with birds. So when they got divorced, their kids became the bridge between them, connecting two worlds that operated on opposing rules of physics.

My brother, David, my baby sister, Natalya, and I were shuttled back and forth between homes every two days. What was permitted in one house was treason in another. What was eaten at one table was forbidden at the other. Their homes and their rules existed on different planets—but more than that, their realities did too. Neither of them seemed to be able to actually *see* what was in front of them, or who. Neither of them listened to what we asked for, what we needed. Neither of them seemed to realize they were operating completely from their own projections, that the children standing in front of them, theirs, were actually real.

We existed to serve what they needed.

A few years later, my dad remarried and things somehow . . . got worse. With this new relationship, I felt iced out, manipulated, and controlled. Meanwhile, my dad did very little to protect his first three children; instead he begged us to please help him not get another divorce. He now had new children, a new family, and a new need for us to exist was handed down to us—to smooth out the kinks with the woman he'd chosen to marry. Like "good" children, we tried, but it so often felt as though our existence was the very thing putting pressure on his marriage. And when we didn't help, because we couldn't, we were blamed.

The marriage ended anyway, but the blaming didn't stop at the divorce. I'm *still* made to feel "bad" for sharing anything about how this person *still* treats us, which is why this section is only a few sentences long.[24] I'm expected to stay quiet, stay silent, protect everyone else—except for myself.

There's an incredible amount of emotional abuse and trauma that comes from being raised by people who seem to see the world as completely revolving around their own perspective. Anything that isn't theirs is wrong, impossible, untrue—including feelings, needs, desires, pain.[25]

---

24 Your girl isn't trying to get taken to court—especially since this person keeps threatening to . . .
25 Without armchair diagnosing, it's safe to say there're a LOT of not-okay and pretty abusive dynamics goin' on here.

Anytime I've acted in ways that aren't in line with how I'm being told to act, I'm informed that I'm "hurting" those I love most. For most of my life, I believed it—and let myself be controlled by it. I didn't want to hurt anyone! But staying silent is what made it easier for it to keep happening. Hiding and excusing behavior is what has allowed for harm to continue, for my little siblings to not be allowed contact with me.

So now I'm finally learning to protect myself, acting in ways that keep *me* safe, instead of worrying so much about how anyone else feels about it. I'm learning to surround myself with people who celebrate, love, and uplift all the parts of me that I've been told are "shameful," "controversial," and "dangerous." I'm done being told that being me is wrong.

It isn't until very recently that I've gotten here.

And I want you to know that you're not alone if you've ever felt trapped by "loyalty" to your family, if you've ever been told not to "air dirty laundry," to keep secrets, to protect the very people who hurt you. You don't deserve to sacrifice yourself for someone else, and you don't deserve to feel like who you are is what causes someone else harm. You don't owe anyone *anything*. No one can tell you what to say or not say about what happened to you. A one-sided contract is void. You're allowed to share and process with others, allowed to have people be there for you, allowed to let the pain be visible and give it some light. That's how we heal. Keeping things in has never helped anyone.

I was in a yoga class the other day, and the teacher ended with this thought[26]—"Before you ask for healing, ask yourself if you're willing to let go of all the things that make you ill."

---

26   Loosely translated because it was in Spanish.

As we invite the stuff that's good for us in, we've got to be okay releasing what isn't anymore.

And anyway, the best revenge is living a beautiful, thriving, love-soaked life.

But back to my childhood, *before* **I could protect myself:** My actions belonged to my parents, and my purpose was to be useful to them.

I filled in all the gaps they left gaping—inside our family, but also outside of it. The doorbell would ring and it would be me sitting with the guest, the landscaper, the date, the accountant for up to an hour as my mother took her time descending the stairs. It would be me smiling and softening the blows of my father's dismissal, his bad joke, his inattention when we were out at a store, a restaurant, running into a family friend. It would be me soothing my little sister's nightmares, figuring out how to get home from school, holding my brother's hand through heartbreak. No one ever asked me what I needed, and I didn't expect to be asked—*is that you, oldest daughter syndrome?*

I wasn't allowed to mess up, to flail, to make a wrong move. It felt like I alone was holding the family together, and I'd drop them all if I did. So I didn't.

But I was drowning, and nobody knew.

Especially my mom, who struggled more than most to pay attention to the world around her.

Mami is known as one of the most beautiful women from her country, a legacy all her own. Hair like a waterfall, eyes full of faraway visions, she's climbed snowy mountains barefoot, knows how to take any seed and make it green, and can turn any space into a sanctuary. Her boundary pushing, her taste, her softness—these are all things I am because of her.

In her Facebook profile picture, she's in head-to-toe cheetah-print silk,[27] long strands of leather dangling from her wrists echoing limbs dangling from a thick branch of a big tree. She's a wild thing that absolutely no one has ever been able to tame (although they've tried). I love that—and it also made being her daughter kind of a nightmare.

She went on juice fasts, was a pioneering raw foodist (*"Seriously, Mami, is that raw corn?"*), and if she wasn't wearing stilettos, she just didn't wear shoes. Her dancer's arches would skim the floor of shopping malls, supermarkets, and sometimes even our school, on the days when she remembered to pick us up.

The people she invited to our house always smelled like compost and never wore shoes. They dressed in organic hemp clothing and always left their shirts unbuttoned. Many things changed dramatically for my family in the years that would come, but back then, my mom only wore designer clothing, and she refused to let anyone but the valet park her blinged-out Range Rover, leaving her six-inch YSL shoes behind in the car.

She shipped containers from Bali full of outdoor beds and painted doors, installing a beach in our backyard,[28] complete with a light installed to look like the moon. She opened a private studio space and covered the ceiling in upside-down

---

27   No lie.
28   *Dump* trucks full of sand.

paintings. She started her own jewelry line, covering big, black fossilized shark teeth in diamonds and emeralds. She took Mayan textiles and made them into chic floor pillows. She was entirely unwilling to participate in anyone's expectations of her.

Which, hello—this whole book is about being brave enough to do that. But with her it was different, at least to me, from her daughter's perspective. It didn't feel brave as much as like she just wasn't there. Her life revolved around herself, as if she'd forgotten she'd birthed children, forgotten she now had bills to pay, forgotten that none of us could simply sustain ourselves with air.

As an adult, I get it. She'd married my dad as a kid, used him as a dad, never had a chance to become her own person under his control. She was rebelling. She was acting out. She was individuating. But unlike most teenagers, she had three children, and a lot of post-divorce money.

We were on a family trip in the Moab desert, red marbled stone standing like giant slabs of raw meat across the horizon. The four of us shuffled our feet through the pink sand, marveling at the natural arches all around us, me, my brother, and my sister running in and out of all the curves. We snuck through a tiny passageway to find an expanse of desert, a lone circular stone in the middle, with a little entrance. In front of it stood my mom, just staring. We ran up to her, giggling.

"Whoaaa, cool!" My brother was impressed by what she'd found.

"I'm going to live here one day." Mami kept staring.

My siblings and I looked at each other. "What?"

"This is where I'll live." She didn't look at us.

"But . . . you'll leave us?" My sister asked the question. I grabbed her tiny five-year-old hand.

"You won't need me. I'll be happy here." My mom left us to walk inside her new home.

My sister started sobbing. My brother had tears falling down his face. All I felt was anger.

I was her daughter, we were her children—and it felt like we weren't enough to stick around for. I did my best to console my siblings, to try and be the parent we didn't have.

But I wasn't a parent, so even there, I felt I had failed—and I felt angry, all the time, that I had to be confronted with that.

One weekend morning during high school, I was at Mami's house and opened the fridge for something to eat before a long run. As usual, it was something between a mausoleum *and* a museum in there. A bunch of containers with stuff that could be sprouting, or rotting, or literally still alive; I never knew. I saw something I recognized at least, and it was my favorite— my mom's cashew oatmeal dough, a pale-colored glob of fat, sugar, and carbs.[29]

I ripped a piece off with my fingers, chewing what was essentially edible playdough. I realized I was starving, and kept ripping off pieces until I ended up eating the whole brick. Oops.

29   Finally!

I ambled around the house while my body digested, letting my little sister stay sleeping in my bed, but an hour later, I was starting to feel a little strange. I stared at the Burmese masks that hung on the wall and sensed that they were staring back. I ran my fingers over the giant tusk my mother had found on some other faraway excursion, and the smoothness of the enamel tasted like cream on my fingers. I sunk myself into the blue chair she'd upholstered and felt myself sinking into some kind of crushed velvet universe.

My head was spinning, my heart was pounding, and my mouth was incredibly dry. I must be dehydrated, I realized. I went back to the kitchen and downed some water. It was getting later in the morning, and the sun would be too high if I waited any longer for my run.

I set out of the house, feeling my feet heavy on the pavement. But like, really heavy. My legs felt like tree trunks, the effort to lift just one absurdly enormous. After a block or two, I sat down on the sidewalk and started blinking my eyes. The sky looked different, and so did the sea. I'd drunk so much water, dehydration couldn't be possible. But my mouth was still dry.

After a while, I got up slowly, continuing to walk. Was I okay? Yes, wow, yes I was. I started running again. I felt light now, my legs like little wings. But then the trees I passed started to look funny, almost alive in a human way. I realized I'd been talking to myself. I sat down again. Blinked. Got up and kept running. I did this for the entire run.

I felt strange, bloated, and far away from myself.

It wasn't until I came back home, chugging more water in the kitchen, that I glanced at the now-empty container of beige I'd polished off earlier and noticed something I hadn't noticed before. Tiny specks of green. Little stray stems and leaves swimming at the bottom of the container.

"*Goddammit, Mami!*" I hissed.

There was only one person I knew in the world who made their edibles with the entire plant, throwing everything in to not "lose the *spiritual essence*." There was only one person I knew who was stashing a marijuana plant in a closet, learning to bake with it so she could sell her raw cacao balls laced with THC as a new business endeavor.

I knew by now not to touch the containers in the freezer, as I'd almost eaten one of my mom's weed chocolates the month before, but the one I'd chosen that morning had been stacked with all the regular food she made in the fridge, food my eight-year-old sister had access to. Food she would have been eating if I hadn't swallowed a two-pound breakfast two hours before.

"Oh, you'll find this hilarious one day," my mom said after I'd stomped up the stairs to her room and declared that she'd drugged me, a *child* (I made sure to harp on this part), and now here I was drooling over myself on a Saturday morning when all I wanted to do was go for a run.

Yeah, I was a bit overdramatic, but I was incensed.

I didn't even drink or smoke weed! I hated feeling out of control, but what I hated even more was that my dad was taking me to lunch and I'd have to pretend to not be stoned out of my fucking mind the whole time. I couldn't tell him, or anyone.

What if, with everything else, the world decided my mom was unfit to care for us?

It took a few years, but in the end, she was right. It's hilarious now, but that's only because I'm safe, I'm okay. Back then, I felt scared, neglected, and forgotten.

Which all makes sense because Mami needed help. She struggled a lot to function in the ways society needed her to—as did I, it turns out—and because I was so focused on performing my role as "perfect daughter," it was expected of me to be the one to help her. After all, this was the role she'd been given by her mother, and her mother before that.

Aunts, uncles, friends, and family members kept telling me, "You're so smart! You're so good at writing! Help your mother."

I hated that they said it. I didn't want to anymore.

I'd asked, warned, begged for the ideas to stop, for the spending to stop, for the eventual financial catastrophe that awaited her (and therefore us, her children) to be stopped.

But I couldn't stop her, so Mami ended up spending all her money in that time. All of it. And there had been a lot.

And not just her own. She'd stolen my and my brother's bar and bat mitzvah money to fund her brother's business idea.[30] Money that our friends, family, and community had given to us in little envelopes with our Hebrew names scrawled on them, money that was meant to help us step into adulthood with the support of our community. She didn't tell us that she took it all, and we didn't find out until we needed it, but it was too late. It was all already gone.

---

30 Not even a good one. It failed.

"Financial trauma" was always something that felt shameful, like it wasn't allowed to belong to me—I, who had grown up in a waterfront castle, a millionaire's view all my own.

But I lost the castle, the view, the sense of calm that mornings looking out for manatees provided.

When I tell someone that a global megastar now lives on top of the tree where my sister's placenta was planted,[31] they think all sorts of things. They definitely don't think of poverty, of my mother's closet filled with designer tags of silk and linen memories turned into blurry descriptions up for sale online.

They don't think of her with a food-less fridge, of smoking cigarettes to stave off hunger, of foodstamps and sleeping in the car on the side of the road. They don't think of all her artifacts she'd imported from Indonesia, India, and Tibet now strewn all over the Everglades, buried treasure across barren backyards—or stuffed inside the walls of bodegas, when Mami could afford them. She spent any last dollar she had to board her stuff, move her stuff, keep her stuff.

"For the house I'll have again one day," she'd say as she fingered her carved wooden statues, her jewel-encrusted animal horns, her handwoven pillow covers—the ones she designed herself.

Multiple leather jackets, all designer, all thousands of dollars, rolled up into pillowcases.

"I'll visit the mountains again, and it'll be cold."

---

31 My mom gave birth to my sister in the bathtub. Under the tree was where that placenta went.

Dozens of platforms, stilettos, skin-covered boots. "I'm not dead yet."[32]

When she left the castle of my childhood, she decided to make her own, a palm-covered pathway to the little huts that made my room, my brother's, and a small garage protected by the life-size wooden horses she'd imported from somewhere else. She eventually lost that castle too.

Over the years, I started picking up her habits. I walked through the world and collected things in my memory, and just like her, I began collecting things in real life too.

I've spent years carrying my treasures, just like my mother. From my dorm to every house, apartment, room I've ever lived in. Boxes of treasures stuffed in closets, secrets sewn into strings of beads.

To give it up would be not only to give away my history, but also this possibility of an imagined future—a world in which I'd have a home to fit these things into, a world in which I wasn't worried about money, war, climate change, or whatever horrible disaster was on its way to happen next. A world in which I wasn't constantly buzzing with terror that everything I loved would be taken away from me, like it had been for my mother.

I've lost a lot throughout my life, but the biggest loss came on December 14, 2022, when I learned my brother, David, had, like so many things, been violently taken from me. He was shot in his home, the apartment he'd so proudly just bought himself, by police officers.

All of a sudden, I knew this imagined world I'd been fighting to keep for years didn't exist, and it never would. All those

---

32   Fair.

treasures didn't mean anything. All that stuff was noise tamped on top of pain.

He left, and he was never coming back. This is the truth that cracks me open still. There's nothing in my bins filled with beaded bracelets and linen bedsheets that will bring him back. There's nothing between the pages of my hundreds of books, or the letters written in my dozens of diaries, that will deliver him—gently, wholly, not even in pieces—back into my hands.

For years I've been holding on to fears that were so much less than what actually came true. For years I've been obsessing over pain that had already happened—fears that were handed to me, fears I hadn't chosen—from generations of parents who'd passed on pain to their children, grief and loss, like their parents had done to them.

This pain, these fears—they were never really mine to begin with, and what if I didn't want them anymore?

Recently, I went down into the basement where all my stuff had been stored since my brother's death. I opened the zippers of the bags they'd been carefully folded into and immediately pulled back from the smell. Black mold laced between bubbles of water along the tulle of my favorite dress. My royal blue gown with the sweetheart neckline, velvet with an extended collar that wrapped around my neck, was now a stiff, moist brick of blue, impossible to pull apart, white clouds of mold lining its folds. Flowers of frothy green sprouted from the bottom of the cashmere coat my mother had given me for the cold. The oversized leather jacket, quilted silk with silver buckles, that

I'd saved for two decades, was now sprinkled with holes eaten through by fungus.

Dead pieces were now filled with life that was feasting on their fibers, that were turning it all into dust. All of it impossible to save. Impossible to hold on to. Impossible to even touch. My stomach dropped and my throat knotted. The loss didn't stop.

I imagined my brother then, beneath the ground, in a coffin my dad picked because he said it looked "distinguished," just like David was. Imagined the green and brown and black mold that inevitably now sprouted from his skin. Life creeping back into his body, all the fungus and bacteria making him their home. I then imagined him as dust instead, a few pieces escaping the gravesite, sneaking their way back into the stars.

Back home, my family is still grieving.
As I write this, I'm sitting in a stone courtyard, lemon and orange trees breaking the sky to offer me shade. Hanging between two of them, a colorful threaded hammock swings in the breeze above the grass, and I hear the birds singing along to the tinny music of a neighbor I can't see. I take walks along cobblestone streets in the morning, passing parks with curling iron benches and ancient trees. I buy boots that look like a fresco, I buy a cape with a jaguar painted across the back. I cut my hair even shorter, wear the same jeans for weeks in a row. I'm trying to write, but it's difficult. In this land of endless inspiration, I feel nothing.

I wake up every morning with new stones in my chest, a heart-shaped organ filled with cement.

David was just killed a few months ago, and after being back home for a little while, all I could do was leave.

I hear the echoes of an old voice, the one that tells me I'm a terrible daughter. I'm disappearing again, abandoning my family when they need me most. My parents lost their son, and my little sister's future is flipping upside down in the aftermath. I'm a call away, a flight at most. I know this, they know this—but the feeling persists. I'm failing at something, perhaps the most important thing.

My brother is the only other person in the world who lived through my stories. He was the one whose hand I held, the one who processed it with me, the one who validated my intense reactions to my parents as an adult. As much as I felt like a Bad Daughter, I'm certain he felt like a Bad Son. He isn't here anymore, but in so many ways, he's more here than ever. It's only because of him that I've been able to move through everything in the last year, all thanks to his celestial support.

The healing in my family is starting to happen, slowly. It peeks out of some phone calls, messages, times when we're together, over the table at dinner.

Mami, in the last few months, has all of a sudden become much more present. She now answers her phone, asks me questions, listens to what I say.

"Happy Mother's Day!" I sing through the phone, me in Mexico, her on a break at her job, mangroves and scaffolding behind her. She's wearing a blue baseball cap, pearls dangling from her throat, her ears. No shoes, as usual.

"I'm so happy I have a job where I don't need to wear shoes!" She giggles.

We both know she's been kicked out of apartment buildings, gyms, and stores for not wearing them.

"I'm so happy you love your job!" I say, beaming. I can't believe it—to see her smiling, in a good mood, and confident at a job is so healing for me.

This is all we'd wanted from her, needed from her—and now she was doing it, giving it her all. It was everything I could ask for after years of feeling like, as her daughter, her stability was in part my responsibility. I felt free.

Today, she's working at a state park giving kayak tours. She loves her job and sharing her devotion to nature with others.

"I put them on a kayak and send them on their journey, and they always come back smiling and in a better mood when they return," she tells me as we FaceTime. "By the way, you look so happy and so beautiful! Well, you always look beautiful," she smiles at me. She says that a lot these days, no matter what I'm wearing, no matter how much I weigh.

"You too, Mami. The prettiest kayak tour guide there ever was."

"I wanted to tell you something." Her pretty slanted eyes, the ones she's always felt self-conscious about, look at me under her cap. "I wish I'd spent more time with you guys when you were teenagers. I know I spent a lot of time with you as chiquititos, but as you grew, it stopped being the same. I love you so, so much, and I don't know how to put it all into words, but I know I made mistakes."

My heart softens. It's so rare I get to see my mom open up vulnerably. I feel close to her.

"I miss David so much," she continues. "I just wish I had had more time."

"I miss him too; it hurts a lot."

We look at each other, a mother who lost her son, a sister who lost her brother. A daughter who's hearing her mother acknowledge the pain she caused her for the first time.

"I have to block the pain of losing him to keep going, to not fall apart every moment of the day—but there are certain things that are unblocking. I keep thinking how I wish I'd been more present. The three of you, my children, are my greatest gift, and have always been. You're so perfect, exactly as you are."

She isn't finished.

"And I want to thank you, Ariellita," my mom continues. "It's because of you, because of the way you've pointed out to me all the things I needed to change, that I am changing. I had no idea. I couldn't see them. I never knew. And it's because of how you communicated, how you reflected me back to myself, that we get to continue healing our relationship. That's all I ever wanted with my mother, and I'm so blessed that because of you, our relationship will be different than mine was with her."

I guess in a way, all the things that made me feel Bad were the very things that allowed us to have something real.

My dad and I have been healing too. When my brother died, Papi opened, like a vessel that had fallen off the shelf and cracked into a million pieces all over the ground. It was so intimate I almost couldn't look. For the first time, I got to really see what was inside him. It was beautiful.

For weeks, I was terrified of losing access to that, to him.

I thought back to when I was a child, when he'd lift me onto his feet to dance, me trying not to hold on so tight that I'd lose him.

And yet, two months later, all the pieces were glued back together—cement, superglue, anything he could find that would make sure he never cracked like that again.

I felt like I'd lost him too.

But then a few months later, I opened my phone to a text. It was a picture of an old diner, red pleather stools and linoleum checkered floors. Croquetas and empanadas in a case by the window, the waitresses who greet you with "mi vida, mi amor." Enriqueta's.

"Every time I'm here I think of you, a baby in a car seat on top of the table, me ordering my pan con bistec and cafecito. I love you <3"

I taught him to say those words to me, those last ones. He uses them now. It means the world.

Walking with me down the tree-covered streets of Mexico City just a few weeks earlier, he paused to look at me. "I'm proud of you," he said.

I cocked my head back at him, confused. I wasn't doing anything except walking next to him. What could he be proud of me for when he'd never said that to me out loud?

"I don't say it enough, I know. You've always been such a perfect daughter, and I never tell you. You deserve to be told. We all deserve compliments, I just never thought you needed them. I realize that you do, all of us do."

I hugged him.

"Thanks, Papi. I'm proud of you too."

As a kid, I had no idea how severe my mother's neurodivergence was or how her traumas had affected her. When she was married at nineteen in a country she'd just arrived in after escaping war, she didn't know any better but to disappear into her music, her classes, her seminars, her spirituality. And once she finally found her voice, her strength, her power, she wasn't going to let it go, even if it meant dragging her, and all of us, down with it. I didn't know how much of a bad mother she felt she'd been.

Because, of course, we can't talk about being a Bad Daughter without acknowledging the Bad Mother who, through our own birth, we created. The Bad Mother who is shamed and guilted for not disappearing with a smile inside her role, like what's expected. The Bad Mother who dares question if becoming a mother was the right thing for her, or her children. The Bad Mother who, in all likelihood, has her own history as a Bad Daughter too.

How do we as Bad Daughters reckon with our Bad Mothers? I suppose we must first begin by reckoning with ourselves.

I couldn't recognize that my mother's brain, what made her so creatively brilliant, was also what made her a "bad mom"— what made her late, made her angry all the time, made her impulsively blow through her money. I didn't understand that her inattention and inability to sit still for two seconds, why she morphed and transformed and struggled in social settings, talking for hours in circles on topics that no one else cared about, was just because her brain worked differently.

She didn't know it, and nobody knew enough to tell her. A beautiful woman is seen as beautiful first, and sometimes that's all anyone decides to see of her. My mother has always been strange, quirky, and very different, but not many have looked much deeper than what she's looked like.

This whole time, she just believed she was bad, carrying the weight of the "bad" mother all on her own. It isn't until NOW that both of us are realizing there was so much more to the story, so much neither of us could understand. Society had always shamed people with brains like hers, and perhaps worse, didn't bother understanding them when they belonged to women.[33] She'd always thought she was an alien on this planet, inhuman in her experience, and she didn't understand why.

All of this context doesn't excuse or invalidate what I suffered because of it. But it explains it. It holds it. It can expand so much further beyond it.

I think I understand my father better now too. Despite his piercing wisdom and presidential presence, he is actually really sensitive. And as a man, he's not supposed to be. So he shuts off everything—everything—until all that's left is a stone wall wrapped in dark skin and a charismatic smile. My father, who, even now, thinks he can tell me what to wear and grabs me by the elbow to cross the street, loves me so deeply he can't

---

33 For real—hardly any research has been done on ADHD and autism in women and girls. National Autistic Society. (n.d.). *Autistic women and girls*. https://www. autism.org.uk/advice-and-guidance/what-is-autism/autistic-women-and-girls

even handle it. So he avoids being too close, avoids asking questions that will lead to an actual conversation, avoids anything that might bring out how he really feels or that is beyond his control. He spent so much of his life building successful businesses—not for the fame, or even the money, but for our family. That was his real reason for doing everything and anything, the best he could, with what he knew, with what he was taught.

The men in my family, theirs is a legacy of power, of leading their communities, of resilience and survival. They were, and continue to be, remembered and beloved by so many. They built Sephardic synagogues wherever they landed, hired those that no one else would. They couldn't be emotional, they couldn't be vulnerable, they couldn't be anything other than stone walls wrapped in dark skin and charismatic smiles.

And my father, well, he's now so much softer than they ever were. So much more self-aware. So much more willing to look—even if it takes him years and years (and years). Between the generations of my siblings, I've seen my father transform into a completely different dad—one who listens, hugs, and even pays attention sometimes. He's learning. He's changing. And I hope he never stops.

I'm still learning too, still figuring out what my relationship is to my parents, my history, the legacy of my family. I know that I carry all of it in me, the light and the dark.

So much of who I am is because of who I come from. And yet, so much of who I am is because of who I've shaped myself to be.

The key is to be willing to look. To be willing to get messy and dirty and deep—not just into the pain, but into the joys when you find them. It's actually pretty easy to point to what hurts—to stare at it for an entire lifetime, even—and blame it. The hard part is looking at the beauty and the power we now have to not just not create more of it, but also go so far beyond it.

It's easy to blame our parents for everything from our past traumas to the struggles we face today. I spent years unable to talk to my mother without my ears ringing. I spent years fighting for the acceptance and validation of my father.

This blame can also be complicated, filled with guilt, shame, confusion—at least, that's been my experience. It's way easier to point to the past and say, "*It's because of youuuuu I'm this way!!!*" and bang against the walls like Godzilla.

What takes some finesse is to actually dig beneath, around, and through all those feelings and discover the pieces of ourselves we learned from them that we actually love (yes!!!), honoring them, while also accepting that even though there may be pieces of our story that we wish we could give back, we can't, so we may as well find compassion for our parents. At the very least, they kept us alive. Whether they did the caretaking or not, whether you even know who they are or not, ultimately, if you're reading this, the bare minimum requirement of parenthood was met. You're alive.

You have the power to decide how you'd like the rest of your life to go.

I'm still figuring shit out. The pain isn't over and done with, and I *still* feel (a lot of) anger toward my parents, but now, gently, and with space—it's turning into compassion, understanding, and an even deeper love.

A huge thing that's helped me? Boundaries.

In some cases, it's been smaller things, like knowing how long phone conversations need to be with my mom before I unravel (three to five minutes if I can sense she's not present, fifteen to twenty if she is). It's been getting clear on my expectations for my relationship with my dad—recognizing I'm an adult now and can remove myself from any situation in which I'm not being treated with respect or care. It's been about understanding what he has to offer—and loving him for it—but never expecting more. It's also meant setting some bigger, more permanent boundaries, like cutting off my stepmom for good (a scary step I took that has been one of the greatest acts of self-care I've ever given myself. Go me!).

I've looked for the ways that I can have the best moments possible with each of my parents, in the ways that they feel most comfortable, from doing activities and projects with Mami to asking for logistical life advice from Papi.

And so this is what I've begun focusing on—all the ways in which my parents shine.

I've started highlighting the ways in which they *do* show up, the glimpses of presence, kindness, and gentleness, so that they know I see those parts of them and can celebrate the special people they are. They smile and feel appreciated; in return, I feel more understood.

It's a two-way street, these relationships, and I'm not a kid anymore. If I want an adult relationship, I've got to show up as my adult self too.

And in order to show up as my adult self to my relationship with my parents—which I care about deeply—I have to set myself up to win. I don't like who I am when I'm triggered around them. I'm impatient, quick to judge, and sometimes even unkind. My nervous system needs what it needs to stay calm, and I am learning how to give myself that so I can show up as my best self and keep myself safe.

All our parents—no matter how wonderful, how shitty, how absent—are doing the best with what they have, with what they've been taught. Even if their best isn't great, even if their best is not what we deserve. It may not be an example of healthy love, but it's how they know how to express love and embody the role of parenthood, giving us what they think we need in order to survive.

What parents don't realize, certainly mine didn't, is that for the most part, those tools they learned from their upbringing are exactly what keep us simply surviving instead of actualizing, what keep us buried in cycles of generational trauma. But there's compassion to be had, too, because, although they may never see it that way, those were just the tools that were handed down to them, the only ones they had.

I have tools, tools they don't have, and tools they may never have, to navigate the difficulties that have arrived in my life and even so, and as horrifying as it is to realize, I am BOTH my father and my mother to my dog. I am impatient, neglectful, codependent, obsessed.

I am everything I swore I would never be, but of course I am, because it's all I've known.

Parents can only give us what they know, what they can relate to. They can't whip up a new style of loving if they've never had it or never known there was another way.

Is there a way on earth we can find compassion for the years of imposed dress codes, the body comments, and the shuffling into certain careers? The criteria for an "acceptable" partner, the curfews, the haircuts? The food going into our body, the calories leaving it, the size of clothes we wear?

Actually, yeah—if we can see that this was our parents trying to protect us.

It's intergenerational. This didn't just start with our parents, and it's not going to end with us. We can take that pressure off ourselves, because it isn't fair, and it isn't ours.

It doesn't mean we're failures, it doesn't mean we're terrible, it doesn't mean we shouldn't have kids—it just means we're human, sorting through hundreds, if not thousands, of years of trauma, history, and the things our ancestors have passed down through the generations. We can hope to break a cycle, maybe even more than that, and give new generations the tools they need to continue breaking more.

The true healing with my parents has come through having a perrhijo—my dog son. It's come through the endless nights of not sleeping, sifting through poop to understand why he's sick, paying for expensive training and late-night emergency vet visits, chasing him around the house so he'll stop eating the furniture. It's come through recognizing my own impatience, my blind spots, my selfishness, my inability to pay attention to something, anything, for hours and hours at a time. Turns out, I'm a lot more like my parents than I thought.

And guess what???

I even left the cabinet open for the dog to get toys out of recently, not even realizing he inhaled AN ENTIRE PACKET OF CBD TREATS . . . and I didn't even notice until my partner held up the empty bag. Of course, my reply was, "This will be hilarious one day." Truly like my mom, after all.

My dog is hyper-attached, anxiously codependent, and reactive toward strangers in the home.

This is partly because of his genetics, but partly because of the way I'm attached to him, my fear of him being away from me, my inability to handle his howling, of hating when he's uncomfortable, of hating when I'm uncomfortable even more. I don't have the skills yet to give him what he needs—but I'm trying, I'm trying so hard. I work with a dog trainer (for a while, I would literally sob during sessions; it's embarrassing, but here we are), I have a therapist, and I work through my responses with my partner.

I have the tools to do something about it, and, just as important, the desire.

When I tell you I thought I'd be an enlightened mother, I am not lying.

I've spent years in therapy, read books, written articles, done "the work." I lived in communities where children were raised alternatively, preached the philosophies, helped bring them to life. I swore I'd learned all the lessons from my upbringing, from my world. I swore I was ready to raise a child who was fully enlightened.

And yet.

HAHAHAHA.

I am now fully responsible for a creature for the first time, and it's not that I'm a terrible parent—I'm not—but the fact remains that I have raised a dog that needs a *horrifying* amount of dog therapy (which I am giving him!!! But still).

IMAGINE IF HE WERE A HUMAN.

Poor kid.

I can't beat myself up over it or expect I'll change overnight. The fact is, I don't have a human kid, but if I did, they'd be a resilient, brave, and complicated snuggle monster—just like me, and just like my dog.

Parenting is a struggle, but there is no such thing as a bad child. There is only a child in the environment they exist in. There is no morality, no deviance, no ill will that a child develops on their own. They become who they are based on where they are planted, how they are watered, and where the sunlight warms their cheeks.

I didn't thrive where I was planted, so I had to find new gardens. And when there were none, I created them myself.

But it isn't just enough to find somewhere new, or the thing that works. You must protect it.

So I'll say it again: There is no such thing as a bad child.

The cool part is, as an adult, you get to say no, you get to ask for support, you get to not come home for holidays if it doesn't feel good for you. You get to be with who you want, dress how you want, and eat what you want. You get to be a sex worker or a pharmacist or a freelancer.

You get to reject the burdens that were never yours or choose to keep carrying them forever (I don't recommend that, though; it's no fun).

Regardless of your culture, your family background, or where you live, you get to make the choices that are right for you. Yeah, there may be a lot more to unpack for some folks than others, but that's the jig. Blaming things outside ourselves isn't helpful. We don't even have to understand those outside things. We don't even have to fully understand our pain. We just have to acknowledge that it's there and work to understand, and trust in, our resilience. It's our responsibility to deal with what we've experienced, to handle what we've been given. It's not for anyone else to sort out, or for anyone else to heal.

We are the ones who get to decide our fate.

I couldn't take myself to a psychologist or speak up for myself when I was being traumatized as a kid—but now I can. And not only that, I can now also choose to actively heal and work through the shit I lived with. I get to make different choices for myself, and build trust with myself, and show up for myself. I get to reparent myself and be best friends with myself.

This is beautiful!

So instead of feeling stuck in where we've been, we can arrive to where we are.

Some reminders for anyone who's a child to someone else:

1. You do not exist for your parents. You exist for you.

There is nothing wrong with you. There never was anything wrong with you.

You are not wrong for not wanting to be who they want you to be. You get to be who you want to be. There is no such thing as a duty to anyone for bringing you into this world. It was the choice of other people to bring you here, and now that you're here, you get to find the things, people, and spaces that make you come alive. There are myriad ways to be successful other than being a doctor or a lawyer, getting married, or having kids. You are here. You are alive. You are wonderful.

That is success itself.

2. You get to take accountability for your own life.

You don't get to blame your parents for being the way you are, for feeling stuck, for not getting help, for making choices that aren't right for you.

You're the grown-up, and that means you gotta act like one. You've got to own yourself, accept yourself, and make choices in an act of love for yourself. You can go to therapy, choose healthy relationships, reparent yourself, and give yourself everything you weren't given as a child. This isn't anyone else's job but yours.

3. It's up to you to surround yourself with people who see you and celebrate you.

If your family isn't that, find other people who are. The world is big. There are billions of people, and no two are the same. Your family isn't the touchstone of humanity or the blueprint of human connection. You get to make those up for yourself. You get to explore and discover the spaces that accept you wholly, without an agenda, without wanting you to be anything other than the beautiful being you already are.

Chosen families are real, valid, and worth investing in.

4. Boundaries are beautiful.

Your job—the only one!—is to show up and take care of yourself (and creatures of any species you've committed to taking care of[34]). Anything else is a distraction or a bonus. It's never a requirement to spend holidays with your family, to have daily phone calls, to go on family trips. You don't have to dress differently, hide your interests, cover your tattoos. Your belly deserves to be as big as it wants to be, regardless of what your family says. Your life deserves to be big, too—and you're the only one who gets to define what that means.

Protect it at all costs. And that means that if it's ultimately in your best interest, you're even allowed to cut people off. You don't belong to anyone who doesn't embrace and celebrate you.

5. You are responsible for your role as an ancestor.

You aren't responsible for *your* ancestors—for your parents, even. They are responsible for you. You can't change, heal, or fix how they've responded to life. It is not your place, and it was not your world. They did what they had to. They survived so that you could.

---

34   And if you don't have what you need to take care of them, to find other ways for them to be cared for.

Your job is to take all that and dance with it. Find the ways that joy moves through your body, locate grief, talk to anger. You are responsible for this world, and the one that comes after.

6. Decide what kind of ancestor *you* want to be.

What world do you want to gift to your children, your siblings, your community? What wisdom are you holding that the world deserves to hear? After all, you are already an ancestor, holding this world for all the life that has yet to come. The pressure to be chasing an individual goal, dream, or mission, to become a higher, more enlightened version of ourselves—this too isn't ours. It's a rebrand for separation—of community, of the earth, and ultimately, of ourselves.

The ambitions that have been placed on us are entirely irrelevant. We might spend our whole lives measuring up to them, chasing them, even reaching them . . . then realize it was never going to be enough. Because nothing is enough if there's a separation from the reason we're doing it all to begin with. Nothing is enough if we've lost the connection to ourselves.

Our only purpose is to care for the world we've inherited, to live from it and live with it the way humans always have.

Blame, guilt, shame—these are all feelings that exist when we are focused on the tiny details. When we grow up in a world that tells us, constantly, that we are not enough just as we are.

We used to just be. That was enough.

We used to just breathe. That was enough.

It still is. We still are.

BAD

LOVER

"Vas a matar a ese animal de tanto tocarlo."[35]

—*Pilar Quintana*

---

35   "You're gonna kill that animal from touching it so much."

The first time I made out with a boy it wasn't because I wanted to. Or rather, I wanted to—it was the only way I'd get all the boys in my middle school to leave me alone—but it wasn't because I *desired* to.

John had asked me to be his girlfriend at a house party. He pulled me aside, some beads of sweat forming where his forehead met his basketball buzzcut, and said the magic words every girl my age was supposedly waiting for: "Will you be my girlfriend?"

I pulled away, panicked. "Um, I don't know." I was too young, I thought. I wasn't ready, I thought. Papi's going to kill me, I thought. "I might be too young," I told him. "I'm not sure I'm ready," I said. "I need to ask my dad."

I turned around and ran to the car that was waiting to bring me back home, sliding into the back seat and feeling my thighs stick to the leather. I was wearing my yellow miniskirt, so tiny I worried my pubes might poke out of it, and I was sweating. I had no idea what I was going to tell Papi. I was terrified as to how he'd react when I told him—which, of course, I would. I didn't trust making a decision like *dating* on my own.

Papi allowed it, with a long list of conditions I can't even remember, and the next day I said yes to John and emailed him Usher lyrics, deciding I was in love—mostly because I thought I was supposed to be.

I let him kiss me on the lips because I knew I had to. That's what being a girlfriend meant in seventh grade,[36] although I refused to open my mouth. A wet, slimy tongue was in no way getting near mine.

This refusal did not sit well with the other boys in school. They said I was "holding out," denying a man his rightful dues. If you said "yes" to being a girlfriend, it seemed to mean your body belonged to someone else now. These were the rules, and I was breaking them.

My very first relationship, and I was already named the bad lover.

John and I broke up before seventh grade ended, and by the time eighth grade started I'd heard he'd made out—tongue and all—with my friend Carla over the summer. I was furious. We'd dated for months, had barely just broken up! He'd told me how much he liked me, but the moment someone else was willing to do what I wouldn't, he chased that instead. I felt disposable.

I realized, a little heartbroken, that it didn't matter who I was or how much someone claimed to like me—it only mattered what I was willing to do. Fine. My overachieving good-girl

---

36 This was iterated and enforced in many ways, although no one had ever said the rule out loud. Even so, all the girls knew to obey it.

conditioning kicked in. If that's the way it was, then I could play the game too—and win it. We got back together, and I decided we'd date so the open-mouthed deed could be done.

This was the first time I took what I wanted from a man, and it would also be the last time for a very long time. I grabbed his clammy hand, exasperated, and pulled him into a closet. I was thirteen and the music was loud enough for no one to know we were in there, even though I knew everyone at the bar mitzvah would find out anyway.

"Okay." I looked at him square in the face. "Let's do it, then." He looked back at me confused. I turned my lips up to him. "We're gonna make out." I sounded confident. I was terrified. "Really?" His eyes grew wide. He smiled like he'd just won something. I pulled his face into mine, opening my mouth so his tongue could slide in. He tasted sour, like milk left out of the fridge to spoil, but I presented my tongue back to him anyway and kept it in his mouth for three . . . two . . . one. I snapped my face away from his. "Okay! We did it. See you later." I walked out of the closet and knew I never wanted to make out with a boy again.

I didn't feel particularly brave or powerful. I wasn't sure what I'd feel, but I was expecting something inside me to change. I was a girl who'd made out with a boy! But instead of feeling *part* of something—the collective of humans who had done what I just did—I felt even lonelier. I hated it. It hadn't been fun, or exciting, or something I even really wanted.

It had been something I felt I had to do.

And something I felt I had to keep doing, simply because I no longer had an excuse. I could no longer say I wasn't ready—I'd done it. So every day, after that party, he'd stick his tongue inside my mouth, and every day I'd crush my eyes closed and let him.

But one day a few weeks later, after he'd sneezed into his hands and then *immediately* reached his snot-covered fingers into my breasts (without asking, of course), I'd had enough. I broke up with him, for good this time, and went on to continue a pattern most people raised as girls experienced. Succumbing to pressure, constantly. Doing stuff I didn't want to do, all the time. And turning the things I was meant to be enjoying into something I resisted as much as I could. To be a "good" girl-friend, to be a "good" lover, seemed to just mean I was supposed to erase myself for a boy to write all over me instead.

Too many of us have a John. Not because we have a bio-logical bad taste in men (or boys, as was the case), but because we've *all* grown up with heteronormative conditioning and compulsory sexuality.

I was made to believe that my inherent worth was my body—but also, that I couldn't be trusted with controlling it. My parents controlled it, then boyfriends did, and, of course, all the while the state was trying to wrest control of it too. I was supposed to be obsessed with sexuality, like society was, but also . . . I wasn't, because I was a woman. I was just supposed to let society be obsessed with *my* sexuality, and pretend to look the other way while they ran their hungry eyes all over me.

I was supposed to be clueless about how the world looked at me—except I had to know enough to hide it, or playfully tease it, or just surrender to it altogether, allowing boys to take pictures up my skirt—which they did, at all the bar and bat mitzvah parties.

Instead of being furious with them, I was self-conscious, mortified they might have captured my barely nascent new pubic hairs in their pictures. Instead of yelling at them, telling them to fuck off, I felt the anxious desire to shrink, shame pouring its heat all over me. I didn't chase them. Instead, I ran away, helpless, my body being taken from me without my consent.

I was never taught to protect my body—after all, it was made clear to me that it didn't belong to me, and never would. I was never taught to learn what my body wanted, what it might desire. The only protective mechanism I knew was to be there without being there, floating somewhere so far away that I didn't have to feel what was happening to my body.

The twisted thing is that this self-removal also allowed me to create judgment toward myself—being in my body but through the eyes of my parents, culture, and religion, internalizing the shame they all would have put on me. I was living in a traumatized body that had no idea how to actually *access* the sexuality that was supposed to be so inherent to it.

I am *still* unlearning how to not completely remove myself from my body, or from my desires. A lot of us spend more time learning how to go far away than how to come back and be close to ourselves. As much as that protection has been worthy and useful, we also deserve to enjoy these bodies we're in—whatever that might mean to each of us. We deserve to be present with them, to touch them and have them touched in ways we might like. We deserve to never be touched again, if that's what we'd prefer.

But it'd be a while before I got there, before I learned that. I still had more lessons to live through. Over a decade after my middle school make-out sessions with John, I had a new boyfriend, Hector.

Hector looked like a Neanderthalian model. He had skin that drank the sun, big lips, and an eyebrow shelf that declared him MAN. His muscles rippled, and his feet were so wide he could've climbed a tree just using them alone. He was beautiful. And he was attracted to me in a moment when most of the men I'd known at the time wouldn't have been.

I'd just moved back home from Brazil, my hair growing in patches from the buzzcut I'd given myself while living in the jungle,[37] and so I felt lucky—surprised, even, to have someone like him look at me. I no longer looked like the version of myself that had won the hearts (and erections) of all the boys I'd grown up with. And still, this man wanted me.

When we started dating, we had sex. A lot of sex. The first time, he dropped me off at my dad's house, and we tangled our bodies outside on the backyard couch under the stars. Another time, after dancing all night on Calle Ocho to bongos and a Cuban saxophone, we got naked in his dad's pickup truck. It was big and red and parked in public. We liked each other too much to care.

We went camping, and before he told me he had Tourette syndrome, I woke up to him banging pots together in the middle of the night. A new tic had flowered. "It's to scare away the

_____

37   A story for another book . . .

bears," he told me, not meeting my eyes. He may have been embarrassed, but I smiled. I, too, had plenty of my own tics.

A few months later, we moved in together. The little duplex felt like a treehouse, complete with a sunroom where I could put out all my pillows and have space to dance. When we moved in, we had a party, a plant potluck. Everyone brought a plant, and our home was covered in blooms.

There was a gas station nearby that had a secret, entire restaurant inside and a wall filled with nice wines. The counter at the front was filled with croquetas and pasteles with all my favorite fillings: guayaba, mamey, maracuya. I loved living somewhere that still felt like I was living somewhere else. We were happy for a while.

But, like a lot of people, I cried the morning I found out Trump had won the 2016 election. Like a lot of people, he didn't understand why. He hugged me, which was sweet, and asked me why I was so upset, which wasn't helpful.

As time passed, the news cycle got worse. Nothing happened to the president. Nothing happened to the Supreme Court justice. Nothing really happened to the Stanford swimmer. The names from Hollywood started spilling out. Powerful Man after Powerful Man after Powerful Man. All weak. All broken. All abusers. It got harder and harder to sleep next to a man.

Even a man as kind as Hector. He was still a man, after all.

In hindsight, my relationship with Hector did not begin with any kind of perfect timing. I'd met him two months after my uncle had touched me in the kitchen, sliding his hands between my legs with his eyes closed. "Is this okay?" His voice was low, and his face was twisted up in a desire that disgusted me. I was visiting him in Guatemala, a place where active volcanoes pepper the floor and if you stick your hand out the window, you can almost always catch a cloud. As his fingers began to erupt quietly over my underwear, burning as if they, too, were made of lava, my body snapped awake, and I pushed him away. I smiled without looking at him, laughing nervously. I felt like the clouds I used to catch in my hands—perceptible in my nothingness. I stopped being a body and became air.

My uncle had helped raise me, so I offered to make him tea. After the water was done boiling, I took my own cup to the sofa, almost dropping it on my way there. I sat down and shook my head at the weird dream I'd just had while brewing chamomile. But when I looked down at my hands, they were still shaking.

My uncle wasn't the first one to touch me like that. There are a lot of men I remember—friends who slipped their hands underneath my clothes while I slept, yoga teachers who never listened to my nos, ex-boyfriends who I believed still loved me. Men I had trusted, had let close to me, men who told me they cared. There were also plenty of men whom I hadn't trusted, who were just close to me in proximity—men on public transportation, men sleeping on hostel beds next to mine, men who walked past me and touched me violently. These are the ones I remember, but there are many that I don't. My therapist tells me I'm "repressing childhood memories of sexual abuse." All I know is that ever since I can remember, sex makes me extremely uncomfortable and every time I touch myself I cry.

The tears aren't simple. They're heavy and thick with memories I don't understand. It starts at my stomach, right below my belly button. A wall slides open to reveal a deep well. Of what, I don't know. There's nothing to touch but the overwhelm of emptiness. It goes too deep to ever know what it looks like, but I hear it howling. It comes up like a bubble, my nervous system boiling, sliding up my chest, a viscous pool of melted glass that hardens and then, just as quickly, cracks. It sends sharp shards up my throat until sand starts pouring out my eyes, my nose, my mouth.

Because arousal makes me so uncomfortable, I usually don't like having sex. Especially when it's vulnerable and intimate.[38]

Things had been fine with Hector—great, even—when there'd still been emotional distance of some kind. I was able to enjoy sex because I wasn't *too* close yet. But when we moved in together, I could no longer keep one foot out the door. I liked him, and that's when things started to change in my body, when I, once again, found myself trapped in the hairs of the broken bad lover inside me.

We'd be on a hike, at a concert, driving at sunset and I'd suddenly realize our entire time together was spent with me floating, unable to be present, unable to even be *there*. It was hard to listen, to focus, to take in anything he said. I'd spend the whole time looking down at myself, furiously fighting to come back into my body—I could see it! It was right there! But I couldn't. And I felt like a failure. The dissociation had hit so strongly that I felt like a paper doll—no feelings, no motivation, no body to hold on to. It's hard to laugh, or pay attention, or

---

38   Shocking!!

care when you don't know where you are. Often when he would hold my hand, I felt nothing. His fingers slipped through mine like a ghost.

Soon, the dissociation had lodged itself into my skin. I wasn't just far away from myself anymore, I literally couldn't even *feel* myself. I first noticed it when I was on a work trip to LA. I was staying at a friend's house off Montrose. We grew up together, and now he was some big-shot Hollywood producer. (He was just one of the men who would think me sleeping on his couch was an invitation for him to touch my body. I kept my eyes squeezed shut and my body rolled over, praying he'd leave me alone if he thought I was sleeping. He didn't.)[39]

When his friends came over, he turned into an Industry Asshole. All his friends were also Industry Assholes. I'd go into another room whenever they were there. One night, my friend was away, so I took his bed instead of sleeping on the couch. I tried to touch myself, to "get back in touch with my body," as one therapist had told me to do. I lay naked under the sheets and felt them cool on my skin. I ran my hands over my nipples, my stomach, down between my legs. I didn't feel heat or humidity. I didn't even feel a tingle.

I threw the sheets off me and pulled on pajama shorts and a sweater. I left the door open and shuffled myself down the block to the CVS. The aisles were bright when I entered, and I tried to disappear among them as I searched for what I was looking for. I finally spotted a tiny pink vibrator on one of the top shelves and grabbed it, doing my best to pay for it discreetly.

---

39   We're no longer friends.

The vibrator was about as big as my thumb and just as thick. Back at the apartment, I rinsed it under the faucet and didn't even make it out of the bathroom before switching it on and bringing it to my pussy. I heard it whirring, but my skin didn't seem to know it was there. I double-checked to see if it was on and increased the speed. Still nothing. I slumped down on the cold tile floor and cried.

After a few weeks of total numbness, despairing that I'd never feel anything between my legs ever again, sensation *finally* came creeping back. But now, everything hurt. Fuck.

Sex became too painful, and I stopped wearing tampons. Anything that touched me felt like sandpaper buffering raw skin. I tried having sex anyway so Hector wouldn't leave me. I didn't realize that's what I was doing, and when I eventually did, I was too ashamed to do anything different.

I went to multiple doctors. Each one told me I was fine. "Nope! All good here!" Each one told me it was all in my head. "Have you seen a therapist?" (Yes.) And, inevitably, each one told me there wasn't enough research done on bodies like mine to do anything about it.

I googled possible diagnoses, possible solutions. I bought dilators and creams, meditated, masturbated, screamed. Nothing worked.

How could no one know what was happening to me? How could the entire medical industry literally not care enough to do some tests?

Our culture is obsessed with vaginas. Trump had only just recently bragged openly about grabbing them. And yet no one could be bothered enough to figure out how to take care of them, or the humans they were attached to.

I started writing and publishing the experiences I was having because I felt entirely alone. I thought something was deeply wrong with me, and I figured writing my story would at least help me feel like there were words in the world that reflected my experience. I didn't know how many others would resonate with my writing or that so many others had been through the type of pain and terrors I'd had.

I kept writing and people kept resonating. The platforms I wrote for got bigger and bigger, and with time, I became a leading voice in the conversations around consent, pleasure, and agency for bodies with vaginas. I felt braver. I didn't feel alone.

And realizing I wasn't alone, that there were millions of women who felt like I did, millions of women who'd been hurt like I'd been hurt, millions of women who were still hurting like I was hurting, made me angry. So angry I felt like the volcanoes in the land of my mother, boiling boiling boiling, ready to erupt, destroy, spill out onto everything around me at any moment. I could not be contained.

I snapped and lashed out and cut down. I screamed and ran my teeth along the spine of anyone who dared confront me.

I was no longer patient or kind. Men were afraid to talk to me, which I liked.

For the first time, I was starting to feel myself—or whatever me that was underneath all that had been covered by my upbringing, socialization, and the media. I, who had once been so afraid of confrontation and of voicing my opinion that two friends had almost pulled my arms apart when I was a kid as they tried to drag me, physically, in opposite directions, because I didn't want to disappoint either of them. For the first time in my life, I wasn't being a Nice Girl.

I wasn't alone in my anger. All the women around me were beginning to erupt too. Soon, I couldn't open anything without reading the stories of friends, neighbors, acquaintances, and celebrities accusing the most powerful men in the world. We all had stories. We all had the scars.

It was 2017 and the #MeToo movement was screaming from the cells of our collective, and individual, skin. We were a chorus of crackling lava, generational trauma conducting a sonata made of red, blue, and white fire.

I wrote with the ashes of that lava. I became even more popular for my scathing reviews of men in power, for the fear I induced in the ones I interviewed, for the rage I extended to the women who read me and didn't yet feel ready to scream out themselves.

But as time went on, I started to see that as sacred as my fury was, as important, as righteous, as alive, it was starting to choke me. Where once the anger had given me strength, power, and purpose, it was now beginning to weigh more than I had bargained for. It was uncomfortable to be lugging around my fangs and claws everywhere I went. It didn't feel good to see a man and immediately write him off as a predator, an asshole, or someone complicit in my pain.

The anger wasn't making me happy, but it made me free. I began to wonder if there was a way to have access to freedom *and* happiness, or at least freedom without so much pain.

Hector and I had stopped having sex months before. The pain was too great, the pressure too much. I felt broken, having to explain myself, to prove myself, to show I was trying, the bad lover in me wanting so badly to be good. But it didn't work, and he felt totally rejected.

"But I love you," he said to me when I told him I needed to stop. "I'd never hurt you."

Tears spilled down my face as I tried explaining. "It's not about *you* hurting me. My body's just been hurt too many times before. Also—" here I paused, looked away from him. "You could still hurt me. Not on purpose, I don't think. But you could still hurt me."

He looked at me like I'd just slapped him.

"How could you say that? How could you believe that? How could you not trust me?"

"You're a man, Hector."

"What, so you can't trust any man?" He was incredulous.

"I can't trust a man who's not listening to what I'm saying or ignoring how I'm feeling, like you're doing right now."

"But I love you. How could you not trust me?"

I didn't have other words to make him understand.

Deep down though, it wasn't just about the sex. As my career was growing, Hector wasn't particularly celebratory. He was tolerant, and that's all I figured I could expect of him. After all, I was becoming a media darling for putting down men, and here he was, the man I came home to, the man who felt he was bearing the brunt of all the bruising I'd experienced from other men.

And yet it wasn't just me who had been taught the expectations of romantic partnership. This whole time, he thought *he* was failing *me* because I didn't want to have sex, believing that it was his fault, that it was because of him, that he, too, was a bad lover. I started realizing that maybe he also felt useless—the mirror experience of my own. He wasn't getting validated in the ways he was used to, the ways he needed, and this left him unprepared and unable to understand the pain I was in, the trauma I was working through. He thought everything that was happening to me was just because I didn't like him enough, because he wasn't good enough for me. He hadn't grasped that what was happening for me actually had nothing to do with him, and so there we were, in a cycle of pain that neither of us could get out of. He never said any of these things to me of course, but it was obvious that we were both hurting, and we weren't the ones to help each other through it anymore.

We broke up—he couldn't make space for all the new things I was learning about myself, and I couldn't stop being angry at him for it. For so much of our relationship, I was convinced I was a bad lover, and in the end, maybe he'd been convinced he was too.

This is all bigger than both of us. Society puts so much external expectation on relationships—a pathway, a tiered system, an end goal (marriage, house, babies, then . . . ?) We're taught to believe a relationship is in trouble if we're having sex fewer than X times per week. We're taught to believe a relationship is good if we stay in it long enough, if both parties are willing to take the steps required—not of emotional understanding, of communication, or of support, but rather the steps that are expected of us, the engagement ring, the wedding cake, and later, the pregnancy.

I thought I'd have all that with Hector, but for the past fifteen years I'd been *expected* to cater, mother, nurture, and ignore whatever it was I needed to meet someone else's needs. I'd always done what I thought I was supposed to do, regardless of whether I wanted to or not. After my relationship with Hector, I was determined to never fall into that trap again. It hurt too much. I was ready to figure out what I wanted, who I wanted, and how I wanted to be. I was ready to embrace being a Bad Lover.

Could sex be something else instead? By the time of my breakup with Hector, I had become a leading voice in the sexual wellness space with my own sex and love advice column for a major publisher. I was moderating a panel at a conference in an airy Brooklyn loft the first time I ever heard a woman say she hated penetrative sex out loud. She was dressed in thigh-high black boots and a long, sleek ponytail was tied at the crown of her head. A tall, attractive man in a suit was sitting in the front row, holding her purse. I felt immediate shock, like I'd been the one suddenly exposed. Did this man know he wasn't allowed to be inside the woman whose purse he was holding? Did he care? But she was a Pro Domme, and she did not give a single fuck what he thought.

I'd never heard a woman say that before. Could I do that too? Could I really never have penetrative sex again if I didn't want to? To even consider making a choice in direct contrast to what a man might want from me, instead focusing on what *I* wanted, felt terrifying and thrilling at the same time.

I didn't like penetrative sex. It hurt me.

Why was I alone obsessed with fixing it, when the health care industry wouldn't even bother to do some research? If I never had to do it again, I'd be happy. It wasn't something I craved or even something I missed. Why had I never allowed it to be a possibility up until that moment, when someone else proclaimed it proudly?

Because I didn't know that it was allowed.

Even though I write about sex and sell sex, sex is one of the hardest things for me to experience. I don't have much of it. This surprises most people, considering what the internet knows me for, and for a long time, this caused a lot of shame and confusion. I felt like a sexual imposter.

I've written relationship advice columns, profiled dozens of sex entrepreneurs and sex therapists, and dissected culture, and the interconnectedness of identity, in sex. But my own personal sexual experiences had revolved mostly around trauma, dissociation, and pain. I'd made a career writing about topics like anal play, threesomes, and period sex—not because these were things I personally participated in, but because I was forever looking for answers, trying to understand why I was the way I was, trying to give myself, and everyone else, permission to just be who they were, to just like what they liked. I felt so much pressure all the time to be different than what I was that all I wanted was to relieve some of that for everyone else.

For so long I believed my body was my worth, and if that body couldn't be offered to a man, then I was broken, invaluable, forever undeserving of love.

Pay attention to this part, because it's important: *We get to redefine sex to be whatever we want it to be.*

Sex isn't a noun, nor is it even much of a verb. Sex does not require touching, or even talking.

It's a relationship. A conversation between bodies, and a conversation with oneself. Sex is an experience, an energetic exchange. With another, with many, or even with oneself. You can like sex, and you can dislike it. You can want it, and then change your mind. In the landscape of sex, what's been defined as "sex" is just a singular dot on the horizon.

Compulsory heteronormativity means our culture sees heterosexuality as normal, the baseline, the Truth. Heteronormativity says that a penis in a vagina is the way sex should be, the way it is, the way it's always been. It says that anything that isn't that isn't sex—instead, it's perverted.

According to this logic, heterosexual couples, at least, should be having wonderful sexual encounters and experiencing constant pleasure. But so many people have sex—especially women—not because they want to, but because they think they're supposed to.

Much of the time, this kind of sex isn't even enjoyable for 50 percent of the participants.

Not that orgasms are the only signal of pleasure, but straight women have the fewest orgasms out of everyone. This is called the Orgasm Gap—in partnered sex, straight women orgasm only 65 percent of the time while straight men orgasm *95 percent*.[40] So much of being a "good" lover, for those of us brought up as women, has been about making men feel good, giving men pleasure. Any other focus beyond that is bad.

---

40   Frederick, D. A., St John, H. K., Garcia, J. R., & Lloyd, E. A. (2017). "Differences in orgasm frequency among gay, lesbian, bisexual, and heterosexual men and women in a U.S. national sample." *Archives of Sexual Behavior*, 47(1), 273–288.

And what about the men? They've been brought up in a culture that tells them they're supposed to find women irresistible . . . while also kind of hating them at the same time. They're taught to find vaginas disgusting, women's pleasure pointless, and the act of fucking them as a means of power and control, not pleasure. In fact, so much of the pleasure that's derived from men having sex with women seems to come from men being able to brag about it . . . to other men. It's actually other *men* they're taught to find irresistible. It's men they're taught to love, men they're taught to please. (While of course not *actually* desiring men, because that'd be super gay and gross, dude.)

Sex is an extremely confusing experience for *most* of us, no matter how and where you've been brought up, no matter what body experiences you have. It's difficult to give consent or be embodied in sexual situations—let alone ask for what we want—when we haven't ever been given the chance to *know* what our bodies want at all. For people with vaginas, especially, we've never been given the space to explore and figure out what our bodies like, what turns us on. We haven't been taught how to show up with vulnerability to a sexual situation, how to make our needs clear, how to construct an environment that feels safe. Of course so many of us disassociate during sexual experiences—we don't know what else to do.

But we deserve more than that. We deserve to feel pleasure, to feel embodied, to actually participate in any sexual experience we have. And if we don't want to? Well, we deserve that too.

So, just in case no one's ever told you this—you don't need to have sex. You also don't need to want it. Ever.

We live in a culture not just of compulsory heteronormativity, but of *compulsory sexuality*—the belief that sex is something we're *obligated* to participate in, that we should want it, and want it always. That it's a requirement of the human experience, particularly inside of a relationship.

But it's not.[41]

Almost all my sexual experiences with men were because I thought I was supposed to have them. There were very few times that I actually *wanted* it. Beyond the sphere of the heterosexual norm, even in queer relationships, the expectation is sex. The relationship is often measured by how often you have it, and the failure of it if you don't.

That's so much pressure for something that's supposed to *feel good*.

We all have different relationships to our sexuality and to our bodies. No two of us are the same. The periods in my life where I've allowed myself to *not* have sex—mostly by staying single because I didn't know I could do it any other way—have been the most healing and transformative. They've been the most empowering. They've been the moments when I've protected my body and decided what I did, or didn't, want to do with it.

For much of my adult life I preferred being single and not having to deal with all the projections that would inevitably be thrown on me because my job was talking and writing about sex. I figured if I chose to be with someone, I'd eventually have to get over this whole not-wanting-sex thing, acquiesce, "sacrifice" for a relationship, because I still didn't know that I could

---

41   Hiiii, folks on the asexuality spectrum *do* exist.

have a relationship and be celebrated exactly as I was. Was I going to choose to stay single forever just so I wouldn't have to have sex?

Had that been my answer, good for me, but instead I met Bee.

I met Bee on the way to a retreat. They picked me up at the airport in San Francisco, me in a brown leather cowboy jacket and Doc Martens, them with their hair painted three different colors, months of sleeping outside obvious on their face.

My hair was in two braids, my stomach upset and tangled. We were on the way to the kind of retreat you might hear about in cult documentaries, and my body knew before I did what I was about to get into. I watched Bee's tattooed sleeves grip the wheel the whole ride.

The full story is for another book-turned-movie with Taylor Kitsch as the lead, but I'd been working with a coach to the stars (who was essentially an unlicensed therapist) for the last two years in an effort to heal my body and all the anger stored in it. I didn't want to be held back by all the sexual trauma I'd experienced. I didn't want to keep hating men. He invited me to this retreat, and unfortunately, but unsurprisingly, this coach would be another in the long string of men to betray me. He was grooming all of us present, and weeks later, Bee and I escaped, scathed, torn apart, and completely and madly in love. Oops.

After that, I spent about a month in the desert alone, just me and some Joshua trees, as I had a full-on freak-out. I knew I was queer—I had, in fact, come out to Hector years ago—but was I *actually* queer? Was I ready to accept the feelings I was experiencing, and even more so, was I ready to let go of the identities I had attached to for so long?

Bee was nothing like anyone I'd dated before, and it wasn't just the fact that they weren't a man. On the surface, they were everything I'd been taught not to want.

(At the time) they didn't have a job. (At the time) they didn't have muscles. (At the time) they didn't even have a home. They were fresh off of spending the last six months living outside on farms, covered in tattoos and a lot of dirt.

And yet, I wanted.

It was an ache unlike anything I'd experienced before. I wanted it so much.

For the first time in front of someone else, I felt I was just allowed to be—without excuse, without judgment, without needing to prove a thing. My simply being there was enough.

For the first time, someone I was romantically interested in listened to me, asked me questions. They touched me in a way that wasn't compulsion but, rather, as if they were writing a song. They made space for the difficult parts of me and didn't back away from them, instead embraced them. They were interested in doing everything required to move toward a life, and a relationship, that we both wanted.

And none of it revolved around sex.

Yes, connection. Yes, intimacy. But they were the first person in my life to tell me that if all I wanted was to hold hands in bed, that was fine with them.

At first, I didn't believe them. Surely they'd realize it was never going to be enough.

But here we are, years later, and we're still constantly working on what feels right to *us*. Not what society or other people have told us our relationship should look like, but what it feels like to us—the two people in it. Sometimes that includes sex that looks like sex to other people, sometimes that includes sex that only looks like sex to us.

I don't recommend starting a relationship from some deep shared traumatic experience like we did, but the work we've had to do in ourselves, and with each other, to climb out of it has taught me more than any relationship book ever could.

I've learned that a relationship is so much more than sex, because the truth is, a healthy relationship has nothing to do with how much, or how little, sex we have. Usually, the most exciting sex many of us are capable of having happens to be in dynamics that most certainly aren't the healthiest for the long term. They may be exciting, taboo, passionate—but a lot of times that comes with an ocean of emotional distance, space enough to feel desire for the thing that you don't, and may not ever, have. It often also comes along with a fair share of toxicity. After all, movies have taught us that toxicity looks a lot like love, and even though it can be electric, you just might get electrocuted.

A good relationship feels good in your body.

But it doesn't necessarily feel like the electric shocks— which, yes, *can* feel great—or be the kind of thing we're taught to believe in as "love at first sight."

A healthy dynamic has to do with the trust and relationship we have to ourselves, to our own bodies, and how we want and decide to relate to the body of another—and through that body, their emotions, spirit, and mind. It has to do with self-accountability, and the accountability we can offer to someone else, the support we can give them to achieve all their hopes and dreams.

Our bodies are the vessels through which we experience life, and so it makes sense that the more powerful, safe, and trusting we feel in our own bodies, the more powerful, safe, and trusting we feel in our lives. Same goes for when we're with another (or multiple others).

When you're with someone(s):

If you're tense, nervous, and anxious, that's your body telling you something.

If you're sucking in your belly all the time, that's your body telling you something.

If you can't fall asleep next to another, that's your body telling you something.

If you feel guilt, shame, and small next to another, that's your body telling you something.

Sharing our bodies can be an extremely vulnerable thing, and if we're not willing to *actually* be vulnerable and let others know what's happening for us in a moment we're sharing, then we can't expect them to be able to be vulnerable with us back. Our bodies are sensitive animals; they pick up on everything, even if it doesn't yet arrive to our brains. If we're feeling some type of way, we can bet the other person feels it—whether they realize it or not.

It may be past trauma that hasn't been worked out yet, or it may very well be how we feel around that person(s).

The more we create safety for our bodies in our relationships, the more our nervous systems can calm down, and the more all the other parts of ourselves can come out, have space, expand, exhale.

For anyone who's experienced frequent, or major, sexual trauma, this is a moment to remember that you've got to give yourself patience as your body heals. There's nothing broken about you. There's nothing wrong with you. Your body's just trying to protect itself and find a way to feel safe again. That's fucking beautiful, and very brave, if you ask me.

Bee and I work on our relationship . . . a lot. We are constantly reevaluating our communication, our dynamic, how we relate to each other in the journey of relating back to ourselves. Our connection is always changing because life isn't static, after all. This is our agreement, our contract, and quite different from the heterosexual norms I was taught to believe.

With each other, we are building the lives of our dreams. Our collective dreams, sure, but even more importantly, the individual dreams we've each harbored. We've made sure that the foundation of our relationship is built to be the springboard for each of us to fly—ideally, together. But if one day that's not the case, then the relationship will be there to continue serving us to fly in whatever direction suits us best.

Even so, every time Bee and I get into a place of thick tension, I play out our breakup. How we'd divide the dogs, whether we'd stay in the same house for a while, who I'd call to tell the news first. This is . . . not really helpful, or very healthy. But it's how my mind tries to rein in control when it feels like it's lost. Instead of putting my energy into how we can repair, I put my energy into how I can run away and protect myself.

How adorably typical of me.

I put up walls so thick that not even the Incredible Hulk could make a dent. I call it my Berlin Wall—a wartime structure erected so that on the outside, I become bulletproof, impossible to shatter. It's kind of violent, in a way. I am impenetrable, leaving Bee with whiplash as to where I went. Bee used to be the only one who'd make an effort to take a step closer, to reconnect after an argument, a disagreement, or a bad mood. I'd refuse to get near them until they opened up first, apologized, made amends.

But . . . that's not really fair. Like, at all.

So now, since we're practicing for me to *come closer* after conflict, instead of bolting, I muster ALL THE EMOTIONAL STRENGTH I HAVE and put my ego aside (just for a second).

I've had to learn to find a way that I can come closer, even if it's the tiniest, itty bittiest little step. I give Bee a little sideways glance and slowly extend my pinky like it's headed toward something that might burn it.

Bee shifts from their own posture of protection back to their relaxed, open nature and hooks their pinky over mine.

This is how we've learned to repair and step closer when we get triggered.

And even though in these situations my pinky is all I can give, I'm cracking the wall a little. And with one crack, the rest can eventually come tumbling down. It used to feel silly, this pinky holding we do, but it works.

So does having a code word.

We've been using "banana pancakes" before saying something that might make either one of us defensive. "Banana pancakes, I noticed you've been leaving the towel on the floor after you shower. How can I support you in remembering to hang it up?"

"Banana pancakes, I didn't like your tone when you spoke to me like that. It hurt my feelings. Can you try to speak in a softer way with me next time?"

It reminds us that we're on the same team—we have a silly code word, after all!—and makes space to receive a request for modifying behavior.

Verbal affirmation is also a big one for us. We realized we were constantly pointing out all the ways in which we wanted the other to behave differently, without actively recognizing all the ways we behave that we each *love*!

So we have a "plus one" system, almost like how you might reward your puppy for being a "good boy."

"I saw you took the trash out this morning. Plus one!" Here I'll press my finger into their forehead, as if I'm pressing a button, a little dopamine hit of reward.

Sometimes, we'll do something that feels really hard, and we'll ask the other for a plus one.

"I cleaned up all the poop from the backyard," I'll say, my face wrinkled in disgust (jk I would never say that, as Bee always does that job, thankfully. Plus one, Bee!). "Can I get a plus one?" Bee will plus-one me, and boop me on the forehead. I'll feel seen, celebrated, and encouraged.

And we do our best to not make assumptions or control one another. Although, I am *always* inevitably trying to control. Oopsies. But I'm working on it.[42]

My therapist helped me reach a breakthrough moment recently. I've not fully committed to Bee because I'm actually . . . waiting until they're the version of them that *I* want. I've been just sort of waiting around to see who they become on their transition, and keeping one foot out the door just in case.

(That's so fucked up.)

But it's also true. And yet, for the entire time we've been together, I haven't been able to see how manipulative my behavior has been, how unsupportive, and how unhelpful. In a way, it's exactly how my dad has always treated me. I didn't *know* that's how I was acting, but now I do.[43] So I can recognize it, own it, and work to behave differently.

So to add to the piles of communication we already have,[44] we do daily check-ins over coffee and tea, or on our morning walks, to see what's alive for each other, what we need, where we're at. We don't just assume we know what's happening for the other person. We have to ask, talk about it, and listen.

We are constantly evolving as people, and so if our relationships aren't evolving too, then we're stuck in something that probably isn't working for the people we are today. Throughout my relationship with Bee, there have been moments where we felt like BFFs, like relatives, like lovers in a romance novel. Some dynamics feel better than others, but when we *force* the dynamic we want from each other, it definitely never works.

---

42 See page 120!
43 Thanks, Debbie the therapist!
44 Relationships are WORK.

The moment we assume we know everything about another, that's the moment curiosity dies, and so does the relationship. Relationships are dynamic; they are not a static thing—they ebb and flow and expand and contract. Every day is another chance to get to know the person or people in front of you. Every day is another chance to discover something new. Every day is another chance to put aside who they were, and certainly who you thought they were yesterday, and bask in the glory of who they are today.

The relationship I have now has required an enormous amount of upfront investment. It also requires an enormous amount of upkeep—it's a made-up idea that a healthy relationship is an easy one. It's also a made-up idea that you should suffer for it.

There may be compromise, there may be discomfort, there may be big feelings, but there is never suffering. No relationship deserves your suffering—romantic, sexual, creative, platonic, familial, or otherwise. If anything, relationships we maintain should exist to help alleviate suffering.

Ever since I've been learning about my ADHD,[45] my algorithms have been serving me a lot more neurodivergent-related content. Flipping through memes recently, I came across an illustration of a penguin describing the normal fluctuations of autism.[46]

---

45 Highly recommend Aron Croft's Hidden ADHD free five-day challenges, whether you're newly diagnosed or not.
46 For wonderfully stereotype-shattering ASD content, my gorgeous, brilliant friend Rachel Lowenstein is a must-follow. So are Ella Willis and Ellie Middleton!

"Bee," I asked, after scrolling through, "do you think I might be on the spectrum?"

I started reading the memes out loud.

"This one sounds like me, and so does this one. And this one. And this one."

"Well, people with ADHD and autism seem to share some similar experiences."

"I know, but it's like, I relate *way* too much to a lot of the experiences people on the spectrum, specifically, seem to share."

Bee came over to where I was sitting on the couch and took my phone away from me. "Hold on, if we're gonna do this, let's look properly." They pulled up a test from a clinical institute and read me the questions.

"But I don't do that," I protested when they were about to click "Definitely Agree" to statements about obsessions, routines, talking in circles, and extreme overwhelm in social situations.

Their thumb hovered over the button each time, and they paused. "Arielle, you do *all* of these things. I live with you. I spend an enormous amount of time with you. You do all of these things!"

My report came back with high autistic tendencies.

"Okay, Bee, now you do it."

Theirs came back with none.

We spent the morning reading about the way autism can present for females, my head on Bee's lap as they read out the descriptions. I nodded my head to about 75 percent of the list.

"Are you okay?" Bee squeezed my hand.

"Yeah, I just—" I felt startled, a little bit uncomfortable. "Like, what do I do now?"

"Well, you can go through a diagnosis, if that's something you want. It might help."

As of yet, I've decided not to go that route, considering my experience with health care professionals validating my experiences is . . . none. (It's important to mention securing an autism diagnosis for AFAB[47] people is very difficult[48] due to bias, stereotypes, and an extreme lack of knowledge—and research!—in the health care industry around women and girls with autism.[49])

For me, the power here comes from validating for myself that I am, in fact, very much not alone in how I experience life, and how I've always experienced it. It's both terrifying and exciting to realize I'm a full-blown adult having to relearn myself, my strategies, and the way I move through the world. I've spent so much of my life *not* being myself to the world that it's only now that I'm learning who I really am and what I really need.

And it's not just helpful for me as an individual. It's been INCREDIBLY HELPFUL for my relationship.

"You know," Bee said, looking at me, "I'm realizing *so many* of our communication issues have to do with the fact that your brain works differently than mine does."

"Oh, now you're blaming it all on me, huh?" I teased.

---

47 Assigned female at birth
48 Barnett, C. (2023, August 25). "Could I Be Autistic, Too?" *Signs of Autism in Women with ADHD*. ADDitude. https://www.additudemag.com/autism-in-women-adhd-signs-symptoms-treatment/
49 The *DSM-5* diagnostic criteria is based on studies of boys and men, and it's only since 2013 that ADHD and ASD (autism spectrum disorder) are even allowed a joint diagnosis. *eye roll* Johnson, M. (2012, October 25). "New rules allow joint diagnosis of autism, attention deficit." *Spectrum | Autism Research News*. https://www.spectrumnews.org/news/new-rules-allow-joint-diagnosis-of-autism-attention-deficit/

"I just mean I feel so grateful to be learning more about how you work so that I can understand you better, and we can work on developing strategies to relate to each other better."

"You still love me with my neurodivergent-possibly-on-the-spectrum brain?"

Bee smiled and grabbed me for a kiss. "Your brain makes you you. And there's only one you."

They grabbed my hand. "I love the you that you are."

At first, I felt uncomfortable claiming a label that I wasn't sure was mine. But as my new special interest quickly became understanding late-diagnosed autism in women, I quickly consumed enough research studies, articles, and first-person accounts to recognize myself in every single one. I've spent my whole life feeling like I was on the outside of some secret that every other human around me seemed to share. Turns out, I was.

Understanding my AuDHD[50] body and brain has been utterly life-changing for every single part of my life—but it's shed an especially powerful light on the way my body experiences sex and intimacy. In sex, I've always gotten over-stimulated immediately—the sounds, the touch, the texture of the bedsheets, how another body smells near mine—and I didn't understand why. These were all things I knew I was "supposed" to like, but instead, they sent me into meltdowns. I also never knew there was a thing called empathy overwhelm. The moment I heard the term, I knew it was exactly what I felt every day. Many folks on the autism spectrum experience

---

50   A cute lil term for those of us who have ADHD and are on the autism spectrum.

overwhelming and distressing "hyper-empathy,"[51] something that has made intimacy unmanageable for me. I feel every single thing someone else is feeling—always. Forget a lover, just getting on a subway has forever been hell for me. Now imagine if someone's on top of me, looking at me, and trying to get inside me! All I've known how to do is either not participate or pretend I'm somewhere else.

I've masked through every single sexual experience I've ever had, and I had no idea that every time I engaged in sex, I was actually actively traumatizing myself. No wonder—on top of my life experience—that sex had always been so hard for me. The few times I've enjoyed sexual experiences, I've been far removed emotionally—and sometimes even physically—and always in total control. And I'm only just now learning why.

Creating that distance helps me remove myself from myself, but not in an unhealthy, dissociative way. It allows me to step into a role, a character in a fantasy world where I don't have to get attached or feel what the other person is feeling. All I have to do is follow the script with clearly outlined expectations. All I have to do is be present with what they're feeling and respond, something I'm always already doing anyway.

All of this is . . . a lot. But instead of shunning these new discoveries, Bee has dived headfirst into learning all about how they can support me find my way to pleasure. With my own body, but also with theirs—or someone else's—should that be the case one day.

---

51   "Austistic people more likely to feel overwhelming 'hyper-empathy.'" Sheffield Hallam University. (2024, February 5). https://www.shu.ac.uk/news/all-articles/latest-news/autism-and-hyper-empathy-study

This particular piece of Bee's and my journey has only reinforced to me that we are in relationship not to own or control,[52] but to offer as much freedom and support as we can to become our best selves through each other. To support each other through our own processes of self-discovery, and have someone there to celebrate what we find. We don't own each other's experiences the way we don't own each other's bodies or sexuality. We're here to make the path of finding ourselves easier for each other. That's it. And whether that means one day we need to see other people—*Eeep!* Scary for me!—or move on from our relationship entirely, we're both *ultimately* okay with that. The kind of relationship we're building has all the space in the world for whatever's best for each of us, and best for our relationship, no matter what that looks like.

Creating the relationship that's right for us isn't necessarily the kind of relationship we've all seen in movies or read in romance novels. I spent much of my life believing that that was what I wanted, but all that brought me was a bunch of expectations, physical pain, and an overwhelming pressure to perform. The relationships I want aren't based on performance.[53] They're about giving each other permission, authority, and autonomy over our own bodies and lives and discovering with genuine curiosity—and a lot of hard work—how to relate like *that*. That's the only goal.

That's relationship anarchy to me.

---

52 When I'm on my most intentional behavior . . .
53 Unless we're both consenting to it . . . in which case, yes please :)

"Relationship anarchy" is a term used in many poly communities that often refers to a type of ethical nonmonogamy, refuting traditional norms and figuring out what works best for the people in the relationship—but it's more usually applied to romantic and sexual dynamics. However, I've co-opted the term and given it a new kind of meaning that works for me. I use it more to refer to *all* kinds of relationships, including familial and platonic ones.

For example, my partner is the person I am building my life with, the person I wake up to every day and share responsibilities with, such as finances and keeping a functioning home for us and our dogs. Our agreement also includes supporting each other's mental, emotional, and spiritual health—and although it seems we tend to forget this a lot more than we'd like to admit, it isn't actually our responsibility to *upkeep* those for each other. We can support, we can help, but we have other people and other spaces where those things need to be nurtured. Even our sexual experiences and sexuality aren't the other's responsibility—we can share in it, we can support each other to continue exploring and finding what we each need, but we can't be the fulfiller of it.

This to me is relationship anarchy. It's tailor-making our agreement to work for us, not the other way around. Most of us have been taught what a relationship "looks like," and we've been taught to mold and repress our desires and needs in order to fit into that. For Bee's and my relationship, that's where the anarchy bit comes in. We are actively fighting against those expectations and actively creating new ones for ourselves and each other.

A huge part of this relationship anarchy means that all my intimacy is not reserved just for Bee. I maintain a vast, deep, and expansive connection with the other people in my life— my friends, my sister—and that means building a life together with them, too, one that includes Bee, but not one where they are the center.

This is counter to *everything* I'd been taught. Prince, princess, princex—whatever the gender, my partner was meant to be my whole world. They were supposed to be my savior, my purpose, the only person I needed to live a full, meaningful life. But . . .

Bee is NOT my favorite person to snuggle with on the couch.[54] They're also not my favorite person to go traveling with. I much prefer getting in the back of a tuk-tuk, kayaking at sunrise, and dancing my ass off in the rain as I explore a new place with Coco. I much prefer going shopping, doing a pole class, and cuddling with Louise. I much prefer laying out treats and candles on the floor and having an indoor picnic talking about fears and desires with Bry. It doesn't mean I don't love my partner or that we're not compatible; it just means there are parts of me that I want to belong to *other* people, parts of me that I don't necessarily want to let my partner into. Not because I don't love them, but because I have others that I love too.

I create boundaries to allow me the experience that I want. I take myself on dates where Bee isn't allowed to come and put a lot of energy into building my own world that Bee has nothing to do with. I demanded to have my own room when we moved

---

54   Sorry not sorry.

out of New York, and now I have a whole writing studio with a dance room attached, all for me.

I go on trips without Bee—sometimes to visit friends, other times just because I like traveling alone. When my best friends come to visit, there are things I don't invite my partner to, time spent just for me and my friend. Sometimes, Bee even sleeps in a different room so whoever's visiting and I can fall asleep together holding hands after a long conversation under a shared comforter.

Something I hadn't realized until I was in a queer relationship is that it's actually a lot easier to become codependent in that context. Everyone assumes because Bee isn't a cis man that they like to do the same things I do, that they can be invited to things I'd normally just do with my friends. We get grouped together as one—not just because we're dating, but also because we were born with the same parts. Sometimes it feels like because of that, people actually forget that we are, in fact, dating, not just two good friends sharing a house. Although I appreciate the inclusion the people in my life have toward my partner, I actually do not want them there most of the time. It's already hard enough to feel like I have a life separate from my relationship, and I don't want my time with my other favorite people to be melted in with them too.

In my life, I strive to undo the hierarchies I've been taught are inherent.

Bee is an incredibly important person in my life, but they are not THE most important. I don't have *one* important person; I have many in my life, and they are all necessary to my well-being, to my feeling of joy in this life. They are also important to my sense of self—there are parts of me that only come out when I'm with my friends, parts of me that stay silent until I see them walking through the door or at a terminal in the airport. Bee knows this, welcomes it, and even pushes me to consider making big life decisions to center these friendships *more*. They've wholeheartedly embraced making my fantasy of living with my friends a reality, and they are an active participant in helping me get there.

The parts that I do want to share with Bee, those are the parts of me that are both the softest and the hardest, the most powerful and the most vulnerable. These parts require an *enormous* amount of care, and for a long time, I felt like I wasn't allowed to ask for it. Bee is helping me learn that I'm allowed to need them, and that they want to help me.

This is also relationship anarchy to me.

Still, just because I want it, it doesn't mean I don't struggle with offering the same space I want to someone else.

Bee was dressed in a striped oversized short-sleeve button-up and a baseball cap. They were sitting in a chair, tying their laces. They were leaving the house to meet a friend. I moved closer to them, tentatively. Sat on the armrest.

"Can you affirm something for me?"

They looked up. "Of course. What's up?"

I looked down bashfully, embarrassment on my cheeks. "Can you affirm that even though you're creating intimacy with someone else tonight, it doesn't take away from ours? Can you affirm to me that you still love me?"

I felt stupid, silly, ashamed. I'm in my thirties, a sex and love expert according to the media, and here I was, still feeling sprinkles of relationship jealousy. But then I remembered what I tell everyone else—feelings are not wrong. They are never wrong. It's what we decide to do with them that matters. So I let Bee know what I was feeling. Not for them to change or do anything different, but to let them know where I was at and ask for something I knew they could give me—some gentle affirmations.

It can be so scary to create any kind of distance in a relationship—like spending an evening each doing our own thing—even if that's exactly what needs to happen, even if it's exactly what we want!

They held my hand, looked me in the eyes, and affirmed all the above.

As they spent their evening on a friend date, I spent mine FaceTiming a best friend in Australia, then buying some alfajores,[55] my favorite treat, to share with Bee when they got home.

I long ago outgrew the idea that anyone would ever be my "other half," but I swung so far in the other direction that, until recently, I thought the most enlightened lovers were meant to be two whole individuals, hardly any intersections between them. I thought I wasn't allowed to depend on my partner, that that would be unhealthy, codependent, constrictive, but it turns out, to build a life with someone, you kinda have to depend on

---

55   Argentinian sandwich cookie made with maizena, stuffed with dulce de leche and coated with caramel bits. It's . . . the best.

them. Otherwise, you're just building an individual life with someone next to you.

My life wants and needs a lot of individuality and independence, but I definitely don't want to build it alone. On the journey to understand my neurodivergence, I've realized I need a lot of support to function as an independent adult. At first, I'd cry with shame that I needed someone else to help me go through my schedule, that I needed someone to sit next to me while I responded to a text, that I required thirty minutes of Bee's brain *every morning* to talk through everything that's going on in my head from the instant I wake up. How could I need someone *else* to be independent? That didn't make sense; that's not what I'd seen in the movies! But my life isn't a movie—it's my life. And I need a lot more support than most people, and I deserve to be in a relationship that wants to give that to me, that wants me to be as big as possible, to thrive.

And that's something else—I'm big in this relationship. I have strong opinions and loud clothes. I make the decisions that are right for me and let Bee make the decisions that are good for them. It took a long time for me to feel comfortable with Bee's family—for a lot of reasons, but one of them being I just don't have much space for stressful family dynamics beyond my own—and I intentionally missed out on weddings, reunions, birthdays, and retirements. Bee used to feel hurt by this. I'm their girlfriend! Girlfriends come to stuff! But just because Bee felt they had to be there didn't mean that I had to. It was a slow burn, but now when I travel thousands of miles to be at their family events, it's because I've *chosen* to be there, not because it's what expected of me in our relationship.

Bee and I also don't expect each other to celebrate special holidays together, to dress in a certain way,[56] to put on any kind of front or best behavior when we're out together.

I share all this in the hope it'll offer you a new perspective or a reinforcement of what you already believe.

There is no one-size-fits-all relationship. Delete delete delete all that from your mind. It can feel scary at first, but it's also what feels INCREDIBLE!

Because, first of all, you get to decide if you want a romantic relationship at all. There's plenty of aromantic folks who aren't interested, and plenty of people who are just happier doing their own thing. A romantic relationship is not a requirement for a happy life.

Can you say that out loud? (And maybe even scream it!!)

A romantic relationship is not a requirement for a happy life. (!!!!!!)

Now, if you do want a romantic relationship, or are already currently in some, it's *you* that gets to decide the kind of thing you want to be a part of. You get to cocreate a space where you can bring yourself wholly—where you can be vulnerable, and strong, confident, and afraid. There are no rules. None! You get to make them up. Your person or people get to help you.

So what kind of relationship do you want? What kinds of things are important in your life, and how will they remain that way regardless of who you're dating or building a life with? How do you want to show up as a Bad Lover?

---

56   Okay, I do a lot of opining on that front, but I've learned to do it only when it's welcome . . .

Building the relationship of your dreams:

1. Write down your nonnegotiables—not in a partner, but in your life.

A partner should fit into your life and help you expand it, not shrink it. Yes, compromise will always be involved, but this doesn't mean sacrifice. I'm not into sacrifices (unless you're doing some witchy ritual under the moon). You deserve it all, and you deserve someone (or someones) who want to help you get it. Point blank period, no excuses.

If you're into nonmonogamy, don't date someone who wants to be monogamous. If you want kids, don't continue in a relationship that isn't going to give you that. It seems obvious, but once you have a crush, once you're flirting, once you're involved, everything suddenly becomes less obvious. A lot of what-ifs and maybes get thrown around, a lot of internal convincing that maybe, just maybe, you can convince them—but no one should be forced to change to fit into a relationship. You don't deserve it, and no one deserves it from you either.

Better to be clear on what you're looking for and find folks who are compatible with that, want what you want, and can help create your dreams with you.

2. If you're currently in a relationship, consider the things you miss about *not* being in one.

Are there any parts of you that you feel have been lost, buried, gone away? How can you resurface them, letting your partner(s) into that journey? How can you ask them for support?

A relationship is never about being held back. That's not a thing. A relationship exists to propel you forward, wherever it is you want to go. If it isn't doing that for you, it's time to have a conversation and figure out what needs to shift to make that happen.

3. Explore and see what you want to put into practice for yourself.

Have a conversation with your body—ask it what it's trying to communicate to you. And, if you feel safe, bring it up with your partner(s). You deserve to feel good in your body with another, and you deserve to let them know what's going on for you if it's not. They also deserve that.

How can they meet you or show up for you if you don't let them in? How can they support you if you're not letting them know that you need support?

There's lots of references to treating your relationship like a business (have a board meeting! A state of the union! Invest!) but I prefer to think of it as a garden. Having conversations on what in the relationship needs to be watered, pruned, repotted. Celebrating the blooms and their beauty, the ephemeral nature that deserves to be sat in for a while. To do nothing with, except enjoy.

4. Figure out what you need to increase your zone of tolerance for discomfort.

Intimacy, vulnerability, and sex (if that's something you participate in) can be places of discomfort. We can feel nervous, anxious, or afraid of rejection. We can feel like hiding, protecting, and getting defensive instead—that's certainly way easier.

But this place of tension, of wrestling with exposing ourselves (in a good way!) to someone else—this is where the magic and growth can happen.

All this stuff is scary for everyone—*everyone.* I don't care how happy couples look on Instagram or how many times a week they have sex. To have a truly connected relationship experience is extremely scary. Having sex that is intentional, that is safe for the nervous system, that isn't performative and is actually pleasurable takes a lot of work. Intimacy takes a lot of work.

If you've had a relationship to sex anything close to mine, whether that be because of sexual trauma or a neurodivergent body (in my case, both), then sex is uncomfortable. Full stop.

If sex is something you want to bring into a relationship—especially with another—then creating a space and system where you, your body, and your nervous system feel safe is *essential* so that you can move through the discomfort that will inevitably show up. Don't push yourself to be somewhere you don't want to be doing things you don't want to do. Your relationship should feel safe enough that should you enter some discomfort territory, your nervous system feels calm enough that you can either decide to expand into it, or stop completely.

You should feel safe enough to exert your agency in whatever direction you choose.

Before putting this into practice, a cycle Bee and I would get into would look something like this:

Bee would make a move because they know I like a little dominant energy in bed.

I, instead of being turned on, would be taken by surprise because I wasn't expecting it—sending me straight into "unknown" territory and already triggered.

Bee would be kissing me and I'd be thinking, "Okay, okay, I can do this. This isn't so bad."

The kiss might last longer than I expected it to, or their hands would reach for my thigh, and all of a sudden, I'd think, "Wait, what are they wanting to do? Do they want to have sex? Do I want to have sex? Are they expecting me to have sex? But I'm thinking about making dinner and I have to feed the dogs and what if I get distracted? Omg, I'm distracted. I'm not turned on. I'm anxious. Okay, maybe I can work through the anxiety. Breathe 1, 2, 3. It's not working. Fuck, Bee's gonna feel rejected. But I don't want to have sex. Well, we're not having sex. But they're gonna want it probably. *I'm too overwhelmed.*"

Meanwhile, Bee is just kissing me this whole time.

I say it out loud. "Bee, I'm too overwhelmed."

We stop, Bee feels rejected, and eventually they stop initiating. Physical intimacy is uncomfortable for me, so I never initiate.

Our sexual intimacy dwindles to nothing, but so does our desire for each other and our connection.

Now, we're learning to create a container to practice this stuff, not just jump into it. Because, as mentioned earlier, besides my sexual trauma, my neurodivergence plays a HUGE role in the overwhelm (unbeknownst to me until, like, yesterday). Learning more about what my needs are in terms of overstimulation, intimacy overwhelm, and communication— needing everything to be EXPLICITLY spelled out clearly and directly—has been a huge help. So has understanding that the best ways for me to have sex are often to depersonalize the experience, so it's not as intimate and I can feel a bit safer. To practice my intimacy tolerance, we now do fifteen seconds of eye gazing every morning (we're working up to more) so I can safely expand my discomfort. Taking lots of cues from the BDSM world, we have structured conversations about what we want to happen in the space *before* we get into the space itself.

We put time on our calendar (I need at least three days in advance!). We pick a time that's most helpful for me—late enough that I've done everything I've needed to do for the day so I'm not anxious about any tasks, but early enough that I know we'll have time to do our aftercare practices, which usually look like lots of hugs and a movie to decompress together. We talk through expectations—what's going to happen, and for how long. We check in around new boundaries that may have come up since the last time—for example, which parts of our bodies we feel open to being touched or not—and talk through any anxieties beforehand. We create an environment together in our room: candles, music, soft blankets—a few sensory hacks to help my neurodivergent body calm down and not get too overstimulated (blindfolds are great for this too).

It's a fuck ton of work, and sometimes I get self-conscious when it feels like I must be the only person in the world who needs all this work just to be touched. But that's not true! Regardless of our relationship to sex and our neurotypes, *everyone* could benefit from practices like this.

And guess what? Setting ourselves up this way, Bee doesn't feel rejected because I have what I need to show up to the space! I have a plan I can follow to keep practicing being safely uncomfortable, and be more and more okay with the discomfort. And with time, I feel less and less uncomfortable, and closer and closer to Bee, and it feels incredibly pleasurable!

But isn't that what life's all about, anyway? Figuring out what we need to support ourselves through the discomfort of living, of being ourselves, of living out our dreams. It's not just about relationships. Increasing our zone of tolerance for the uncertain, the unknowable, and the uncomfortable is what allows us to lead big, curious, expansive lives. It's what allows us to trust ourselves, to gain confidence, and to take the steps required to be fully *alive* and in love—with the world, with others, and most importantly, with ourselves.

I want that for me, and I want that for you.

And I'll say it again: You're allowed to not want sex. You're allowed to be in a relationship and not have sex. You're allowed to take a sex hiatus, or make it permanent. For some, not having sex (forever, or just for a while) can be THE MOST pleasurable thing.

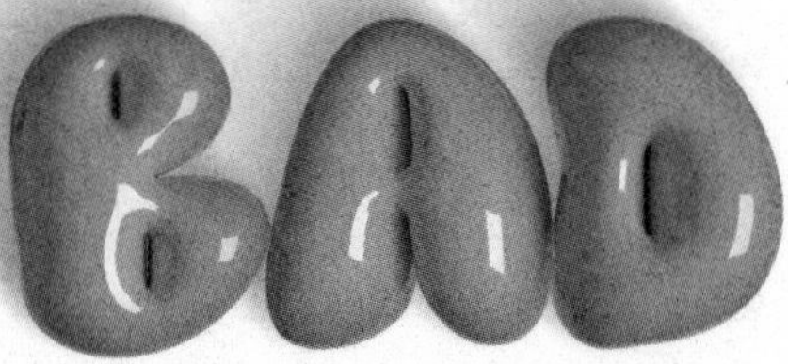
BAD

SLUT

"'I hope you don't mind tea in mugs,' she said,
coming in with a tray. 'I told you I was a slut.'"

—*Barbara Pym*

Contrary to what you might believe about me since reading the last chapter . . .

I'm a total slut, just a bad one.

My whole life I felt destined to remain a "goody-two-shoes" (what girls I grew up with said about me), a "bitch" (what boys I grew up with said about me when I wouldn't have sex with them), and always, *always* "too corruptible" (what a DJ twice my age said while breaking up with me).

As a child, I always envisioned my Prince Charming.

Every night when my abuela was visiting, she'd tuck me in, reminding me to smile while I slept because "you never know when El Principe will come." I was six and already choosing nightgowns with lace, posing on my pillow before bedtime, fanning my hair out, and keeping my head perfectly still as I fell asleep. I'd seen the movies. The princes always come when you're sleeping, and even as a preschooler, I was stayin' ready, bitch.

As people who are AFAB, we get princess lessons not just from Disney but from everything around us.

Even before we get popped into the world there are all these arbitrary attributes assigned to us and random rules to follow.

Somehow, the older I got (and the more physically developed), the more expectations there were to meet *and* the more mistakes to make. The older I got, the less safe it was for me to be loud, to have opinions, to dress in ways that felt true to me. By "safe" I don't mean *physically* safe—although that was always lurking right beneath the surface of their stares—I mean safe from shame. Safe from being talked about, put down, isolated, and ostracized. Safe from being looked at, rejected, ignored. Safe from too much attention, too much judgment, and ultimately, too much power. The world reinforced this, and so did my parents, and school, and boys, and the movies.

For the most part, I did my best to follow the rules. I was obedient. I stopped having opinions. I kept my wants to myself. I covered my body and smiled at anyone who stared. I was nice, polite, and stayed quiet with a smile plastered to my face. I played my Good Girl role really well, for as long as I could.

To be anything else—to be bad out loud—drenched my nervous system, spun my heart in hula hoops, slipped my skin into mercurial waves. It was all *too much*, too risky, too dangerous to be myself.

But no matter how much I followed the rules, it didn't matter. People looked. I got too much attention, which became too much judgment, which became too much power that I didn't know what to do with and that I didn't want. I was told it was my fault. I had a responsibility for looking the way I did. I had to work twice as much as everyone else to be invisible, to not be hissed at on the street, to not be groped by family members. I spent some years crying once I realized that an entire life following all those rules hadn't protected me, hadn't kept me safe—in every sense of the word.

Nothing had.

That's when I realized to be someone in a busty body like mine meant safety from judgment was all an illusion.

SLUTS, A PARADOX

The word "slut"—in English—has had many definitions over time: a lard-dipped rag (true story), a dog, a hard piece of bread, anyone of a*ny* gender who had an untidy and unkempt appearance. To be a "slut" throughout history wasn't a particularly positive thing, but once upon a time, it was no big deal.

Words are symbols, and definitions change over time—context is always what gives them shape. A word without context is just some letters strung together, a sound someone makes with their mouth. It doesn't mean anything. It's only when the word is used with an intention that it can communicate something—an ask, a description, a warning, a spell.

It wasn't until the late fifteenth century that the word "slut" meant a woman with loose morals, and it wasn't until much more recently that it took the shape of anything to do with promiscuity or sex.

Today, most of us define it as a word used to describe a woman "who behaves like a man."

What they mean is—a woman who *owns her sexuality.*

Oh.

So a slut is a woman who gets down, or at least, in theory, enjoys it when she does. What's the problem with that?

Well, a slut may be a woman who is desirable, but now you know that she *likes* sex; she just may not choose to have it with you. She now has the ultimate power to reject you, choosing to have sex with whomev*er else* she wants instead.

Young men have shot up college campuses because of this.

"Slut" is a word used on you the moment you're perceived to have too much power—like when you've chosen a tight-fitting outfit, ignored a catcall on the street, or accepted a compliment. It's meant to be a Very Bad Thing, something to be ashamed of, a warning to keep you in line.

According to society, we sluts have no morals. We're careless and dirty and full of tricks. We'll manipulate you and use you and throw you under the bus to get what we want. *Especially* if you're another woman. Sluts are competitive—we'll do anything to get a man's attention.

We sleep with anyone and everyone and have no standards. To sleep with us is to scratch an itch. We're gross. The only validation we get is from oversexualizing ourselves.

Yet, *also* according to society, sluts are smokeshows. We're the hottest thing, walking around with our perfectly constructed tits tucked into tight dresses, cleavage spilling over like a cookie outside its mold. We pour all your money into the way we look, and might decide to not fuck you anyway. We're fake, superficial, and stupid. We're conniving in our seduction, and we'll trick and trap you into giving us what we want because we're that hot—which, I mean, only makes men sound gullible and sluts sound like scientists.

In the end, a slut is a woman who's too smart, too dumb, too pretty, too ugly, too confident, too shy, too powerful, too forgettable. A slut is any woman who needs to be put in line.

Its definition even changes according to class, especially among women. According to research done by Elizabeth Armstrong and Laura Hamilton published in *Social Psychology Quarterly*, economic inequality drives many of the differences in the ways women talk about "appropriate" sexual behavior, and often, calling someone a slut has *nothing* to do with sexual behavior at all. Go figure.

To someone working class, a slut is more likely to be someone who exhibits cliquey and snobbish tendencies than someone who has lots of sex. In this case, their elitism is what elicits the word. Blair Waldorf from *Gossip Girl*? Slut. Cher Horowitz from *Clueless*? Slut.

Meanwhile, to the wealthier women in Armstrong and Hamilton's research, sluts were defined by those who didn't dress or behave like an upper-class person. In this case, it is the *lack* of elitism and perceived low-class "trashiness" that makes someone a slut. Jenny Humphrey from *Gossip Girl*? Slut. Tai from *Clueless*? Slut.

Even though it was the wealthier women who statistically had more hookups throughout college in this study, the poorer classmates felt they couldn't have gotten away with the same behavior, as if wearing designer clothes served as a shield against stigma. Apparently it helps, because the more privileged women didn't seem to care if their peers-with-less judged them or insulted them—who were some low-class sluts to judge their sexual behavior?

The reality is that "there's no such thing as a slut," as Olga Khazan wrote in her 2014 article of the same name in *The Atlantic*, which highlighted this study. "'Slut' is simply a misogynistic catch-all, a verbal utility knife that young people use to control women and create hierarchies." I mean, judging from the demographic age of people who call *me* a slut on the internet, I'd say it's definitely not just "young" people. It's anyone with a vendetta against someone saying, being, living *too much*.

"Slut" is a word anyone can use against a woman and have it hurt. Let it turn the school, the government, the country against her. Let it take her children, her money, her legacy away. Let it remove her credibility and turn her into just another witch.

And like I said—I had never wanted to be the witch. I'd always wanted to be the princess, but that's a lot more confusing when you aren't white. Everyone I saw on Disney had light skin and blue eyes, even the witches. I didn't have either. I had no idea where in the fairy tales I fit.

I was in seventh grade when Tina slammed me against the lockers and held me there with her fist. Her other hand started prying my right eye open, jamming black eyeliner along its ridges. My eyes watered from all the flinching, and eventually I broke free.

I walked around the rest of the day with one eye covered in black lines of greasy pencil.

I got made fun of a lot in school, but not for reasons you see on TV. The boys thought I was hot, and I got bullied for not trying to take advantage of it. Tina's defense that day for assaulting my cornea was that I had never worn makeup before and she was just trying to make me into someone who deserved the attention—someone who tried.

Remember John from the previous chapter who I didn't wanna make out with? Well, everyone knew about it.

On the way to class one day, a guy in my grade wrestled me into a grip and grabbed my arm, writing "P R U D E" in big thick black sharpie across it. When I finally got to class (late), I hid in the back of the classroom and tried covering my forearm with a big textbook the rest of the day.

There were lots of sluts at my school. People talked about them, not necessarily for the sexual activity they had, but for their confidence with boys and the way they *talked about* sex. Even though almost all of them were considered hot girls, it wasn't a *good* thing to be a slut—but apparently it wasn't a good thing not to be, either.

There was no way to win, although the closest thing seemed to be a formula that involved being sexual with a boyfriend, but not *too* sexual. Not sex, never sex—but make-outs, letting him feel you up, and maybe even *gasp* a fingering or two. The second you gave a blow job, well, now you were a slut.

As an adult looking back, I can cite the Madonna-Whore complex and intellectually unpack all those experiences from my youth, slot them into categories, and comb through them with all sorts of frameworks. But the memories—the *feelings* of doing it all wrong, of disappointing a boy you like, of having girls talk behind your back—well, that hits different.

No matter what side of the spectrum you fell on as a young person—slut, prude, or anywhere in between—it was real. The feelings you had around it are still valid. It's not just research in a peer-reviewed paper or some quote in an article a friend shared. Those experiences are foundational to your identity, to your sense of self, and to your relationship to your inner slut.

It affected me a lot, and so it wasn't until my late twenties that I finally dared to swing my pendulum from Madonna straight into Whore. I wanted to reach the Slutty Enlightenment, that Feelin' Yourself Nirvana that was forever taunting me on Instagram. I wasn't sure how I'd do it, but goddammit I'd try.

I attempted a one-night stand in my late twenties—the kind where you meet someone during the day and then let him pick you up on his scooter at night. We went straight to the beach, our bodies covered in star-dusted sand. We kissed and his tongue felt like wet sandpaper against my mouth, but I liked his West Coast skater style, and the small amount of native in his blood came through his eyes, his long hair. His sweetness kept my mouth open. People walked by, which excited me and made him nervous. He fumbled with his shirt, his body, his decisions. He didn't know where to put his hands. He asked if he could give me a massage. It was bad. We started grinding on each other, and I asked if he could eat me out. "I don't do that," he said. I rolled my eyes and knew I'd never see him again.

We had sex, which was also bad, and when I went to look for where I'd left my shorts, I couldn't find them.

I couldn't find my purse either. Or my wallet. Or my phone. It was four in the morning, and I wasn't going to be able to get back into my apartment or call anyone for help. I was now naked with a stranger who knew I had no one to call and nowhere to go. I shivered. He offered to let me sleep at his place. I had never intended to see this person again, but here I was, getting on the back of his scooter, *again*, this time with nothing but my underwear, driving back to his "apartment." Once we got there, I realized calling it an apartment was too generous—it was a room with a door. The mattress on the floor was the singular piece of furniture, sheets on the bed ripped in multiple directions. I could see all this because of the one hanging lightbulb he had. But the dude was letting me spend the night when I had nowhere else to go, so I just smiled and ignored it. I borrowed an oversized shirt and slid into the bed. It sank beneath my weight. As I lay down, I looked up. My entire body froze. There, right above the door and looking out over the single mattress, was a giant portrait of Jesus's face.

Fuck.

Hoooooow had this happened?

This was supposed to be my first *real* Slutty Adventure—I thought people did this all the time. Now I had been robbed (literally, but also sexually . . . I hadn't had a single orgasm), forced to sleep in the dirty bed of a strange man, *and* he was a Bible thumper. He was a skater boy masseuse covered in tattoos, man. I thought that kept me safe from Jesus.

The next morning, he left me with a book to read while he went to Sunday Mass and I waited for the locksmith: *The Theology and Dangers of Sex Before Marriage*. I cried while I waited outside my apartment in his baggy shorts. When I finally got a new phone, I texted him about giving back his stuff. He responded three days later, saying I was The Temptress the Bible had warned would come after him. I was his sinful temptation, and he needed to use all his earthly strength to stay away from me. Apparently, he'd cheated on his girlfriend "because of" me, and so he couldn't talk to me anymore. For the next few months, every time he saw me in the neighborhood, he'd cross his body with his hands and then cross the street. Goddammit.

I felt dirty, sinful, like a whore. It felt terrible.

But . . . did this mean I was finally doing it right?

I figured I might as well embrace the temptress I apparently was and continue my effort to be a slut. I dated men who had children, men who were queer, men who jumped out of military planes for a living. I dated a couple—although, à la me, it never got sexual and remained purely, and *very*, emotional. I dated a woman who was in an open relationship and took me out the day after her wedding. I dated architects, cinematographers, music producers. I dated writers, professional basketball players, creative directors. I dated founders, software developers, woodworkers.

I bit into each one like the chocolate truffles they were—something different to try inside each of them. But every time, I'd end up putting them back into the box half-eaten. I could never finish one whole. I wasn't sure this slut life was for me.

There were a few other moments of sexual experience, not all as catastrophic as my one-night stand, but close. There were men who wanted to tell me what to do with my body, and worse, men who wanted to mansplain my own experience back to them. There were men who, in bed together, pulled down their pants and touched themselves in front of me, instead of asking if perhaps I'd like to be included.

There was the time I went home with an Argentinian artist, scruffy beard and long necklaces hanging around his broad chest. Much older than me, he had a nose that was slightly crooked in a way that made him look supernaturally masculine, like a rugged superhero, and he seduced me the way I've always thought men were supposed to. Once I was in his bed, he put on my favorite album from Gotan Project, letting the electric violins wrap my body in its tango.

It was dynamic and sensual, the scene filled with swelling bodies and cedar and citrus from the candle he lit.

Until I remembered where we were—in a shitty room he was renting in a weird part of town, all his roommates eating a microwave dinner right outside the door while we danced. We were on his bed, a mattress on the floor, and I let him kiss me. I felt awkward, and he just grabbed my hand and put it on his penis. Instead of exciting me, my body stopped thrumming and just went numb. Then he put it in my mouth. I felt weird about it. He came and I didn't. After, I just grabbed my stuff and walked through the audience on the other side of the door, went home, and never saw him again.

And *that's* the most romantic sex I've ever had with a man.

It was somewhere around that episode that I realized I was *not* having a good time. I had tried being *society's* version of a slut, but these experiences didn't make me feel powerful. I didn't feel like a badass or like I no longer cared what people thought about me. In fact, a big part of the reason I was getting myself into situations that didn't feel right for me was *because of* what other people thought of me—well, what they had made me believe about myself. I thought something must be deeply wrong with me if sex—the most basic of human interactions—wasn't something I was constantly after. All of America was obsessed with it. So were all the different Bibles. Billion-dollar apps had been built around making its access easier. It was this secret, obvious *thing* that seemed to be constantly on the minds of everyone around me. If I wasn't trying to chase it all the time, well, I must be defective.

I had thought being slutty meant you had to always be down for sex. I thought it meant ignoring your boundaries and being cool with whatever as long as you gave "enthusiastic consent." But how could you truly consent when you were confused, when you were pressured, when you didn't even *know* how to say no? I realized that all these times when I had been feeling unsure, scared, and overwhelmed, I had been blaming *myself*. Not the pressure I was feeling from who I was with to do things in a way that didn't feel right for me. Not the lack of sex education and awareness around sexual dialogue and communication that most of us never got. Not the centuries of violent oppression that had woven itself into my skin, its threads itchy and hot and impossible to unravel without unraveling all of me.

Part of me thought that was just the price to pay to own your sexuality, which felt like the most fuck-the-patriarchy thing you could do. You just had to tell your body to shut up, and there, you'd won.

But isn't this what the patriarchy's like, *literal* goal was? To break us away from our own voice, our own trust, our own power so it could control us? I'd never walked away from one of these slut-chasing experiences feeling full, or nurtured, or like I had been offered more than I'd given. Generally, I left feeling even worse about myself than when I had started. How could *this* be fucking-the-patriarchy? I just felt like I was doing it a favor.

All of a sudden I realized *this whole thing* is what felt broken. Not me.

Did that mean the definition of sex positivity I'd been taught was just a big scam?

(Yes.)

Through all of these experiences, I had thought I'd feel *freedom*—finally, I could be a rebel of my gender too!—but it turns out my desire for freedom was just being used against me this whole time.

Plenty of folks mark the beginning of women's sexual liberation as starting in the 1960s with the "Summer of Love," but first of all, here we're talkin' about white women, not *all* women. Second, the "Free Love" movement ultimately wasn't about being truly slutty and free at all. It was about control under *the illusion* of freedom. There wasn't really a rejection of gender norms as much as a new way to reinforce them. How convenient for men to paint a story of women's sexual liberation while pressuring them into a new expectation that if they weren't cool with casual sex, they weren't down with the times—all the while making false promises to them that their respect and dignity would remain intact. They were promising the end of the slut.

Back in 2013, Joni Mitchell gave an interview to the UK's *Uncut Magazine*, not down with the '60s "Summer of Love" culture.

"Free love? It's a ruse for guys," the musician told the mag. "There's no such thing. Look at the rep I got . . . they made me into a love-bandit. Nobody knows more than me what a ruse that was. That was for guys coming out of Prohibition. It was hard [for them] to get laid before that."

For many men, free love really meant free sex.

Basically, if "good women" waited to have sex until marriage, then in order for men to have sex when they wanted, they had to pay for it (or steal it), the way they'd been doing for centuries. If they could convince women that it was now progressive and "empowering" to have sex, they no longer had to pay.

Another win for the patriarchy.

Women of the time were discovering "to our surprise and dismay, that despite the New Left change in head, shape, hip action and buttons—most of all buttons[57]—that the position of women was no less foul, no less repressive, no less unliberated, than it had ever been," three early Chicago-based feminists wrote in a 1967 essay titled "A Woman Is a Sometime

---

57   The 1960s version of posting a solid-color square on Instagram in support.

Thing." "There was this ethic that it was good for you to have as much sex as possible . . . and you were uptight and hung up if you did not," recalled Susan Keese, a woman who was twenty years old during the summer of '67, living in San Francisco and later in the Black Bear commune, to NBC News. "Some women seemed to be comfortable with that, but I was not. Years later I found out many of the other women did not want to do it, either. We felt like we had to work on ourselves if we didn't like it."[58]

These beliefs are still felt today by plenty of women and AFAB folks in progressive spaces. People assume being "sex positive" means *always down for sex*. That it means *sex is the vehicle for our liberation*. That it means *you're fucking over centuries of progress if you're fucking*. I know I felt that way, like I had somehow internalized my own oppression by not going to sex parties and throwing myself into orgies, by not having sex with strangers I met online or out at a bar.

"I thought you were pro sex," I'd be told when turning down sex after a date.

"Aren't you, like, a feminist or something?" I'd be asked when uninterested in getting felt up after dinner.

Being sex positive means believing sex can be a *positive* thing in your life. It's about promoting judgment-free spaces of exploration of self, identity, gender, and sexuality. It's about creating conversation and tools to increase tolerance around all kinds of sexual desires, including the *lack* of desire. But that's not how the term is often perceived.

---

58   "Free love: Was there a price to pay?" (2007, June 22). NBC News.

The weaponization of sexual freedom is just another way of controlling our bodies and our decisions, just another way to make our yeses and our nos irrelevant. The patriarchy took sexual liberation for women and turned it into women's sexual availability for men.

The disappearance of the "slut" (or her twin sister, the "prude") never happened, because men were never on our side. But we never needed their permission.

I realized, during all this time, I'd been placing the source of the slut's power in the hands of men. It was only through having sex *with them* that I'd gain True Slut Status. It was only through sucking *them* off and giving *them* orgasms that I'd rack up my points. Nah, little dudes. It was time to take all that power back.

I had to remember the reason I wanted to be a slut in the first place.

Sluts have fun. Sluts go after what they want. Sluts don't give a shit about your rules. Why was I putting myself through mediocre make-outs and conversations I didn't want to have? I'd fallen into the trap of not having fun, not actually doing what I wanted, and giving a shit about what would or wouldn't make me a slut.

I gave myself **New Rules**, which will perhaps serve you too:

If something isn't fun, don't do it. If something doesn't feel good, don't stick around. If someone wants to kiss you, and you're not 1,000 percent clear that's what you want to do, try leaning out of the "maybe" as a yes, and see how you feel when you lean into the "maybe-means-a-no" instead.

If something does *feel good, say so.* Be unapologetic about it and ask for more. Get out of your head and drop into the feeling, and if *at any moment* it stops feeling good, stop. Communicate what's going on, and slow down or stop. Immediately. Even when a car's in cruise control, the moment you hit the brake, it slows down. You don't owe anyone anything except respect.

And speaking of respect, this applies to our own bodies first. We're not taught to respect where our nervous systems are at or what triggers them. Don't ignore the signals and push past your own boundaries. Make space for your body and all its needs, listen to them, and make decisions from there.

Our only job is to own it all, or at least be on the path to.

For so long I thought my body was broken because of the way it responded to physical intimacy, to vulnerability, to sex. I know what my body's been through—I mean, I was there—but somehow it's so convenient to ignore the trauma and blame my body instead.

Sex just doesn't feel good for me.

I feel *a lot* of things, but I'd never use "good" to describe it. Weird, right?

Turns out, not really.

My nervous system freaks out from intimacy, let alone the sexually physical kind. Considering the history of my body, this makes sense. As you already read, I cry *a lot* during, and especially after, sex. Not sweet little tears rolling down my cheeks post-coitus, but wailing sobs that I choke on. So much snot it slips into my mouth. Body convulsions that may be confused for a seizure.

All of this while I'm totally naked—with someone I know well, or not. My tears have no filter.

It's powerful, it's overwhelming, and—it's just the way it is.

I used to be incredibly embarrassed about this. I was terrified of being found out. I didn't want to freak anyone out, or make someone uncomfortable with my body's responses—even though the point of sex is *for* the responses of the body. I just believed it was only for the *Cosmo* magazine–approved ones.

The wounds, the discomfort, the conversations I need to have around sex—it's all real vulnerable shit. A lot comes up for me with intimacy, attachment, and sex, like they do for anybody. I have *my* particular set of instructions that work for my body and nervous system, but you have your own, and there's no one else in the world who shares your Operations Manual.

We each have one, and all the fears, trauma, joys, experiences, and desires our bodies have had are written in it. We may not even be aware of the ways certain moments in our lives have impacted us, but our bodies are, and it's all in the Operations Manual. Even though as humans, we all share the same fundamental wiring, every moment we experience—starting from the womb—our whole systems are being rewired accordingly. Just finding our On button, or accidentally tripping over the wires and causing system failure, is unique to each of us.

There's no such thing as being "good at sex." The best lovers are those who listen, who are curious to learn your body and know there's no other one like it, know that the same body will be a different body tomorrow to explore. Although, growing up,

I didn't know this. I thought there was just a "good" and "bad" way to do sex.

My generation grew up at the height of *Teen* magazine. *Cosmo*, *Seventeen*, and *Elle Girl* were all laying out the Top Ten Tips for a flatter belly, a better blow job, a more flattering wardrobe. Nothing was ever okay as it was—it could always be improved. The Silicon Valley dudes putting butter in their coffee think they invented biohacking, but it was the glossy pages of teen girl magazines where efficiency, productivity, and discipline were born. There was a way to do it right, and a way to do it wrong. Being in a body, let alone being in your body *with* someone else's, was never about acceptance, compassion, and joy—it was about following certain steps to keep it all in line. It was about staying skinny, making your boyfriend come, and hoping one day your smiling face might be the one featured in the footnotes of one of their pages.

This all paralyzed me. I didn't want to make a wrong move and be rejected. There was no way for me to be present if I was constantly worried about "messing up." Like many AFAB people, so many of my sexual experiences had been nonconsensual, confusing, and uncomfortable. I didn't feel safe, let alone present enough to be curious or playful or brave.

Instead, I turned stiff and scared, my eyes going big as paper piñatas, body hollow and lifeless dangling in pieces over the bed after I was cracked open and all the candy had spilled out.

I had trouble communicating what I was okay with and what I wasn't, and didn't even yet know how to differentiate between doing what I thought I was supposed to do—whatever my sexual partner was asking of me—versus what I actually wanted to do (usually just be held and talk).

Sex is incredibly vulnerable, and the kind of casual sex most people are having isn't built on true intimacy. It's more often built on performance, on dissociation, and on blocking emotion (which doesn't mean that it can't be fun). But for true intimacy to blossom, we need vulnerability and trust. Without trust, which takes time, intention, and lots of communication and boundary setting to develop, we can't really be vulnerable. Without vulnerability, we can't be emotionally intimate.

As intimate as we might assume all sexual acts to be, most folks out there are having sex that's actually built on being as non-intimate as possible. This isn't necessarily a bad thing. Non-intimate sex can be super helpful, super valid, and super affirming when done *intentionally*.

There's a big difference between *casual* sex and *noncommitted* sex.

Casual sex, to me, identifies an experience where there's little to no communication around boundaries, limits, and needs. There is no contract around regulating the nervous system or even desires. It's kind of an "every body for itself" kinda deal. That doesn't mean confusion, triggers, or intense desire won't come up—they probably will—there's just no playbook the parties have come up with to navigate any of it. Meanwhile, noncommitted sex, to me, identifies an experience between folks who are in no way committed to each other beyond the sexual experience. It does, however, identify that there's a commitment within that container. It isn't casual—there's work being put in to take the bodies, identities, and nervous systems of all parties involved seriously. There are conversations had and cues put in to identify the boundaries of the container. There may be frameworks used to ensure a process of beginning, middle, and end (in which case "end" isn't orgasm, but aftercare).

Having one-night stands is awesome if you're clear on your boundaries and what you want out of the engagement. It's usually less awesome if you're not.

Meeting up with someone from Tinder or Grindr whose name you don't know is perfectly reasonable to scratch an itch, express yourself, or feel someone touching your skin. It's less reasonable to assume that whoever you're meeting up with wants the same things you do unless you talk about it.

Fucking your hot neighbor whom you've been crushing on for months is fantastic—if you're clear on where they're at and what you're both interested in having from this experience. Fucking them and finding out *after* that they have no intention of checking in on you or connecting with you further *fucking sucks*.

Having some play partners—people who only exist in tightly sealed containers as sexual partners, often consistently—is a wonderful way to explore your desires, develop your communication skills, and lean into different sexual dynamics with people you trust and have built safety with.

Role-playing is an excellent way to bring back performance and some emotional blocking into sex in a way that's healthy and intentional, allowing everyone involved to tap into parts of themselves that they might not often express. It's a wonderful way to engage with gender identity, gender roles and dynamics, and power play, and even though there are certain tender parts of ourselves we may be blocking, it's a pathway to ultimately unlocking other parts of ourselves that we perhaps *didn't even know* wanted to be seen.

Still, role-playing with a play partner is not necessarily intimate. They don't have context of the rest of you, or your life, outside of sex. In that case, if you end up going for a coffee after to talk, *that* may be the moment of deepest intimacy between the two of you, letting someone else into other parts of your life. Meanwhile, role-playing with a primary partner, although it brings in performance, can actually be *extremely* vulnerable and intimate because they have context to put you into. You're being seen and witnessed *in* your explorations, instead of just arriving in them with the rest of you a blank slate.

Sex with a sex worker is another great example of non-intimate and noncommitted sex. They won't be showing up with their vulnerability, the same way someone you've just met won't, but as professionals, they'll show up with boundaries and trust, ready to hold the space for you to dive deep into your own self so that *you* can have an intimate experience with yourself. Sex workers are the perfect avenue for intentionally noncommitted sex, the perfect space to explore yourself in a container without judgment, without future dynamics to worry about, and full of process and safety.

For cis women having sex with cis men, the pleasure gap is a tragedy, as we've plenty discussed. So why has the marker of sluttiness been having sex with men, *not* having an orgasm, and being left feeling confused, used, and like shit after?

I decided, not anymore.

I didn't need men to validate my identity as a Thoroughbred Slut. I didn't need them to tell me what I was or what I wasn't. I didn't need them to be myself in all my expressions.

I could arrive there all by myself.

This realization changed everything. If I didn't need men to be a slut, well, then I didn't really need men at all.

I didn't need to dress for men, or work for men, or follow men's rules. I didn't need to date men, or end up marrying one, or even cheat on one. I didn't need to be a good girl, or a girl at all.

I could just be me, as I am, a slut.

And, of course, that means *my* version of a slut. Not Nathaniel Hawthorne's version. Not Feminist Instagram's version. Not the Bible's version. My version. *A Bad Slut.*

Being a Bad Slut means I get to define *myself* and my identity. It means I can be okay with where I'm at, not trying to be anywhere else other than right here, right now. It means I don't yet have to know everything I like or don't like, and I don't have to know everything about my own pleasure, either. I can be in perpetual exploration and conversation with those parts of myself, and let others into it, if and when I want to.

It means letting myself evolve when I want to, and letting myself stay where I am when I want to. It means walking with my tits out some days, and covering myself in oversized sweaters on others. It means nurturing my slutty energy and letting it grow into what it wants to be—no partners necessary.

Sex positivity isn't about having sex. It isn't even about liking it. It doesn't really have anything to do with sex at all. Sex positivity is about space—the space to allow anyone to *make the choices that feel good for them.* It's about believing that every body has the right to be a sexual body in the way that it pleases—whether that's alone, with a lot of people, or absolutely never.

Some of the sluttiest people I know never have sex.

Some of the sluttiest people I know are very religious.

Some of the sluttiest people I know prefer eating a great grilled cheese over eating ass.

Some of the sluttiest people I know have sex for a living and love it.

Other sluts don't have expectations, or invitations, or demands of you. If you're a slut, welcome. If you want to be one, well, you're already here.

Being a slut is about wanting what feels good, *whatever* that is.

The lesson in this journey is about listening to yourself, not anyone else.

It's about checking in, creating conversation with your body, and never thinking that you have to do things you're not comfortable with in order to fit some label, title, or identity.

Sluts don't do that.

You wanna fuck?

Do it, and do it safely (of course).

You wanna not fuck?

Don't do it, don't pretend to, and enjoy your day another way instead.

You're now ready to give the middle finger to *centuries* of control and step into your Slut Era. You're ready to throw your hands up in surrender to your inner slut, strip back your skin to expose all the softness underneath, and get sexy—in, like, a sluttily spiritual sense.

You're ready to step into the world as a Bad Slut.

THE BAD SLUT COMMANDMENTS

These are your commandments—and by that I mean, this is what worked for me. Take or leave what you want and don't want, always. All I care about is that you're doing what feels good and right and comfy for *you*.

1. Sluttiness is an energy, not an action.

Lots of people have sex for a million different reasons—many of them not good, or fun, or consenting. Sluttiness is about pleasure and desire and that feeling in your body when you eat something absolutely *delicious*. It's about following *that*— making it your compass, your road map, and your true north— and leaving the rest behind.

Being a Bad Slut isn't about being anything other than being you. It's not about doing things for the cred or following rules someone else made up. It's not about ignoring the signals of your body and pushing its boundaries. It's not about breaking trust with yourself. It's about staying true to your own flavor and moving through the world with the confidence of someone making that choice for themselves. You talk how you want, walk how you want, and exist how you want. You exude your power in the ways your power wants to be uniquely expressed. You don't shape-shift it into something else or force it into a word it isn't. You know that you don't have to have it all figured out or have it all make sense yet. You know you can be confused, be unclear, be learning, and own it with your whole body.

Slut energy is never imposed. It is never prescribed. It's never the same for everyone. The only way to be a True Slut is to be you. It's the Bad Slut philosophy. Welcome, boo.

2. Wear whatever the fuck you want.

Halters, miniskirts, or grandma sweaters, I don't care. If it makes you feel good that day, put it on. Like wearing clogs on dates? Do it. Like the leggings that make your ass bounce? Let's see. Like your nails long and pointy, but scared you'll seem too ratchet? If you're not Black or brown, acknowledge the history of this style and the choice you're making in wearing it. If you're Black or brown, acknowledge that for centuries decisions about your body have been made for you, and make the damn choice that feels good *for you*. Whether stereotypically slutty or not, express your body in the ways that light you on fire and announce *you*, not just to the world, but also to yourself. Burkas are just as slutty as wearing a bikini to the mall—when they're a choice. Choices are sexy. Decisions are hot. Make them, own them, embody them. Let us see you and cheer you on.

3. Pop your gum.

This is more metaphorical than literal, although by all means, if you like sucking Juicy Fruit against your teeth, do enjoy.

Whatever that weird quirk of yours is, embrace it. Whether you like to flip your hair or take selfies in the bathroom, do you. Whether you like to bring a book wherever you go or doodle on a notepad in the subway, do you. Whether you like to not drink at parties, or not go to parties at all, do you. You're allowed to take up space, you're allowed to do things differently, you're allowed to be perceived as an uncommon, or a perfectly common, experience. Ignore the side eyes and keep going.

4. Get the cake, and eat it too.

This one's literal, not metaphorical. To be a slut is to follow your pleasure. It's to follow your senses (again, literally) to what feels good. It's about taking yourself on walks in the middle of the day and buying yourself the cupcake in the window. It's about lighting your favorite vetiver candle and moving your hips to your favorite song in front of the mirror.

Getting the cake also looks like going home before 10 p.m., or ordering a single cocktail and not having any more. It looks like waking up early to have coffee on the porch, and it also looks like staying up all night raging with your best friends while they're in town. It looks like reading in bed or binge-watching your favorite show when you're on your period. It looks like wearing that halter dress because you love it, and being okay with your arm fat jiggling while you wear it. It looks like not wearing that halter dress even though you love it, because you don't like how your arm fat jiggles while you wear it.

Being a slut is about being in your body, your pleasure, and your desires. It's about saying no to stuff that doesn't excite you and learning to say YES to everything that does.

5. Ask for shit.

This means you have to have some *ideas* about what you want first, which Get the Cake is a great practice for. A lot of us don't have this practice, but to be a Bad Slut, you gotta *want*, and then you gotta be able to handle it when you don't get what you want.

You've got to get playful with rejection.

Just because you ask doesn't mean you'll get it—but if you never put it out there, you'll definitely never have it. If you're too scared to get a no, you'll never get a yes. People can't read your mind, so you gotta say what you want out loud, and you also gotta be ready for them not wanting to give you what you asked for. So practice asking for little things, big things, weird things, things you don't even care about. Practice asking, and practice getting nos.

6. Get real nosy.

I don't mean stalk someone else's Instagram—I mean get curious about yourself.

Being slutty is all about curiosity, exploration, and the desire for more. Not just of wanting more, but of *being* more. Being loud, being hungry, being wild, being down. Being willing to get uncomfortable enough to learn new pieces of you—whether that's reading a new book, dancing with a new part of your body, or trying a new self-pleasure technique. Never stop exploring.

7. Demand attention.

Not in a toddler-tantrum way, but in a grown-ass way. You don't have to stand in the center of a room in a ball gown singing a Miley

Cyrus song, but be okay with speaking up. Be okay with being looked at, being judged, being witnessed. Be okay with standing up for something, especially when that something is you.

8. Own your feelings.

There ain't nothing hotter than someone who has intimacy with themselves. Don't pretend you don't care when you do—that's child shit. Don't hide from feelings when you have them—that's also child shit. Don't make someone else feel bad for feeling—*that's* asshole shit. Whether it be attachment wounds, emotions, or triggers, it's what makes us human. Don't beat around bushes or try for "discreet"—get direct. In relationships, stuff comes up. Vulnerability is how we show up for ourselves, and how we can show up for each other. Practice it, and keep practicing, and never stop.

As a Bad Slut, you know that people can't read your mind, so you say what you need to say out loud. You don't have to know exactly what you want yet, or even what you don't, but you communicate where you're at in the process.

QUEER

"I am worried about straight people."

—*Dr. Jane Ward*

"Queerness is the answer. It's your medicine."

I was sitting alone on a rock in the Mojave Desert and this, of course, was the mushrooms talking.

I'd never taken them before, and neither had any of my friends. The others were back in the cabin where we'd covered the floor in pillows and laid out a bunch of snacks in preparation for our potential overwhelm/ecstasy/confusion (??)—we weren't sure *what* would happen. We'd all only microdosed, taken the smallest possible amount, and before I'd even arrived on my Rock of Enlightenment,[59] I'd already had a small ego death, a brief romance with a very prickly Joshua tree, and a photoshoot with a shell I'd found in the sand.

In my sober life, I'd fallen completely in love with someone who wasn't a man and was freaking the fuck out.

As I sat on my rock and heard the mushrooms telling me that the way to process all my traumas was to forever move

---

59   At some point this rock became god in the shape of a . . . rock.

away from the male gaze, I laughed. I cried. I hugged my knees. I crawled back to the cabin in tear-streaked joy, joining my friends as they danced under the stars.

It would take a full year and a half of cross-country moves, *lots* of therapy, and more than a few sexual orientation OCD[60] crises to integrate that desert mushroom voice to know I wasn't a bad queer, but I did it.

Ten years ago I tried coming out to my mom at a sushi restaurant. She immediately started crying. "Why would you choose this?" Her tears fell into her soy sauce cup as she pleaded with me. "You like men. Stay with men. Don't make your life so hard." When I told my dad a few weeks later, he didn't even blink. He just looked at me and said, "You're not a lesbian." I believed him.

For years, I continued dating men with brown skin and big muscles, like I thought I was supposed to.

I was living in New York with Hector when I flew to LA to record pilot episodes of a podcast that never aired. As I sat across from my subject of the morning, her hair spilling out of the topknot on her head, she stopped speaking and smirked at me. "Here," she said. "Let me fix this." Her fingernails were short and her fingers long and slender. They moved quickly. *Must be all that drumming*, I thought. She took the mic I had rigged and moved it, changing all the settings I'd so carefully prepared. I blushed. "Yeah, I guess you're the musician, huh?" I told her, my

---

60   Ugh, the worst.

eyes cast down at my hands. She just smiled at me and kept talking, answering my questions. I felt exposed, like I was the one being interviewed.

After it was over and I was wrapping up my equipment, she asked, "What's your deal in New York?"

I didn't want to talk about New York. My boyfriend was in New York. I didn't want her to know I had a boyfriend. I didn't want her to think I only liked boys. I answered honestly. I hated how it felt. I walked out of her apartment and took a last look at the bed. I wondered what happened there.

The next morning, I woke up in a tepee. It was raining outside, and the wet had seeped in. I heard a bird chirping and wondered where the bird was keeping dry, until I remembered the tepee was the "room" I'd rented, a canvas tent plopped on some guy's West Hollywood backyard, Los Angeles traffic blaring in the background. The chirp wasn't a bird; it was someone's alarm.

I FaceTimed Hector from bed, and the entire call was a fight, just like every call recently. Hector and I were fraying.

It had been a whole year of conversations between us. A whole year of no sex, no intimacy, no common ground to connect over. I asked him to go to therapy, but he didn't want to.

I needed more from him, he felt hurt by me, I was a burden, and he was the problem. I hung up. I thought about the drummer in her yellow apartment, all brown fingers and strands of bleached curls. I missed the calm I felt with her.

I took a cab to Venice to get some air and found myself walking into that celebrity-dusted place where they have affirmations on the menu instead of food. I ordered some mushroom-enhanced purple latte that cost ten dollars and drank it as I walked, palm trees dotting the sidewalks like stiletto heels stepping on sky. I didn't know what it was about the aesthetic playground of Hollywood, or the splash of relief being away from my relationship's merry-go-round of fighting, but I realized I needed something to change. Immediately.

I saw a salon with a sign in the front: First Haircut Free. I walked in and told them I wanted bangs.

As I sat in the chair, the stylist running her hands through my hair, I thought about the first time I kissed a girl. She was tall with slender brown fingers, like the drummer. Her eyes looked like almonds, if they could grow in the Amazon, where she was from. I fell in love with her, but I thought that was just the kind of thing that happens when you live somewhere else, somewhere far away. It'd been five years since that brief romance while living in Rio, and here I was, still not wanting anyone to know I had a boyfriend.

I realized in that moment that what I felt was not a phase.

On the red-eye back to New York I couldn't sleep.

I climbed the five flights of steps to our Park Slope apartment and waited for Hector to wake up. His eyes were still groggy when I said it. "I'm queer." He looked back at me, blinking. "I don't know what it means yet. I don't need to do anything about it right now, but I just needed to say it."

Tears came out as I spoke, but ones that made sense. I felt like *I* made sense now. He looked at me, confused, then laughed uncomfortably.

Three days after I came home, with my new bangs and the word "queer" still unsure and shivering on my tongue, Hector finally went to therapy. When he came back from his session in the late afternoon, the March sun setting over the East River, we had the last big Conversation.

He cited my new "queer bangs" as an argument point. I cited his refusal to read any of the feminist texts I'd sent him over three years. He didn't want kids. I thought I might.[61]

Even so, the care we had for each other was clear. So was our future.

We broke up.

On that work trip to LA, I realized my dad had been right all those years ago: I wasn't a lesbian—I was bisexual.

As a bisexual femme (most days), my sexual identity is invisible to most people, not just my parents.

When I'm alone moving through the world, people assume one thing. When I'm walking down the street holding hands with my partner, they assume something else. The assumptions, always, are wrong. Every time I go out in public, I'm reminded that people can't see me. Every time Bee goes out in public, they're misgendered with every glance. Because society doesn't understand how a masc person with brand new threads of facial hair is holding hands with someone who looks like me, they often get mistaken for my young son (which . . . ew).

Statistically, the queer folks with the highest rate of mental health struggles are bisexual and trans people,[62] who straddle binaries and have to confront their invisibility daily, as well as

---

61   . . . back then.
62   "LGBTQ+ communities and mental health." (n.d.). Mental Health America.

carry around the history of erasure we've experienced. We're forever moving through a world that has no place for us, a world that completely forgets we exist, a world that has no idea what to do with us.

I grew up knowing gay men existed, but that was it. I didn't know I could be gay, or that my being gay meant that I could still like boys too. I thought the only lesbian in the world was Rosie O'Donnell, and she was, as far as my kid brain understood, fat and alone—the two things I was being raised very much not to be.

I didn't even know my tío was gay until I was a teenager,[63] having learned enough about the world that I dared ask. In my Latin Sephardic Jewish family—despite many family members being queer—the only way to handle it, according to them, was clear: Don't acknowledge, don't address.

Coming out to my parents has been a process as long as my adulthood, and because of that, it's made coming out to myself take just as long. I believed them when they told me I wasn't queer. I didn't have anyone else around me to ask, and I didn't know anyone else who experienced queerness the way I did—starting with the fact that bodies alone have historically done very little to excite me.

Growing up, when everyone else was crushing on cute guys, or talking about how hot a girl was, I couldn't participate in the conversation. I had no celebrity crushes, and I never daydreamed about a specific person sweeping me off my feet. People have sexual desires for lots of reasons, and mine only

---

63   I'm so grateful to him for being himself. Without him showing me it was possible, I might still be dating MEN!

came from proximity to power—the position someone was in, the way they carried themselves with confidence, what their affection could gain me—or the genuine way someone's attention made me feel (which is way different than just liking someone from a distance because of how they look).

For a long time, I felt like a bad queer. I came out late, and even once I had, I was always running away from my attraction to non-cis men when it did show up. I felt very attracted to confident masculinity (I still do[64]), and I didn't know how to reconcile that with being "queer." None of it felt obvious, loud, or full of pride.

I didn't tell anyone about my queerness with a rainbow flag waving in the background, or get an undercut after I kissed a woman for the first time.

For me, reckoning with my queerness looked a lot more like wrestling with confusion, intrusive thoughts, and not knowing where I fit. I didn't feel particularly relieved discovering this new part of myself; I felt completely unraveled.

To me, to be bisexual is inherently to be a Bad Queer. It requires expansion, integration, and in our own way, breaking all the rules. It means having to choose, over and over, to center our queerness, to prioritize it in our lives. For many of us, it wasn't as easy as "always knowing," and coming out became a much longer process than we might have liked. Many of us can go our entire lives having heteronormative relationships, and it can be that much easier to shrink our queerness into invisibility, obscurity, and invalidation.

---

64   Now, I confidently know I prefer it on bodies that aren't cis men.

In case it's helpful to hear it:

1. Queerness isn't something to prove, to anyone. There's no checklist to fulfill, no identity markers to express, nothing for you to do except be yourself.

2. The only thing you need to validate your queerness is your relationship to it—not who you have or haven't slept with.

3. There's no right or wrong way to be in relationship with your sexuality, and there's no rulebook to follow. Your sexual (or asexual) journey gets to be all yours on your terms. You're the only one that gets to create it, and you're the only one that gets to invite others in to participate in it, if you so choose.

The spectrum of sexuality is vast. Every single person on it has a different experience, and whether you consider yourself part of the spectrum or not, we can all relate to the compulsory sexuality of the society we've grown up in.

We're all expected to be obsessed with sex. My whole life I thought something was wrong with me that I wasn't. It felt irrelevant, tangential, an afterthought to my experience of being alive. It's never been the center focus, never been the turning point of any decision I've ever made.

In the world of the toxic straights, men are (taught to be) biologically, intolerably, impossibly (!) attracted to women at all times . . . as long as women are thin, waxed, shaved, and perfumed.[65] Men are pressured to be obsessed with them, crave them, desire them so much that goddess forbid he gets a boner (It's your fault! Don't blame him! You're just sooo attractive to him.), and it's now your job to "help him" get rid of it, the pain is *so severe*. Poor guy!

AND YET, as we've unpacked in previous chapters, these very same toxic versions of men don't seem to *actually* like women very much, if at all. They do not seem to care about their feelings, or their needs, or their bodily autonomy. They do not even seem to care about their pleasure.

Which is why Jane Ward's dedication page in her book *The Tragedy of Heterosexuality* is "For straight women." She writes, "May you find a way to get your sexual needs met without suffering so much." Because, out of all the genders and sexualities, it's actually the straight women we've got to pitch in to save. Indeed, heterosexuality for women has been a tragedy, and they deserve support through the perilous experience of belonging to a culture and a community that actually despises them.

There's nothing wrong with being who you are and liking what you like. What's wrong is how bad we're made to feel when we aren't following society's expectations, and how even worse we're made to feel when we *are*.

As someone who loves power, I thought the best way for me to get it was to follow all the rules.

And when the rules, invariably, didn't work, I tried believing my power was my hair, my body, my smile, the only things that DID seem to work. And superficially, sure, they did—but

---

65   Because—oh no!—an un-douched human body!

my real power, the power that could give me the life I wanted, had nothing to do with what I looked like. It was actually in my willingness to let go of those things, to no longer need to be liked, loved, or wanted, that my true power, and therefore my queerness, came to life.

I've found this power (and my queerness!) by holding the hand of my childhood self who loudly wore her lace-trimmed socks and sparkly heels as I now, in adulthood, fill my closet with floor-length ball gowns, rhinestoned jackets with padded shoulders, and pants that flare out into orange chiffon. I've also found it by exploring all the parts of me I was never allowed to show—the inner skater boy that I had to repress when I could only date skater boys, not *be* one. My drawers now get to hold my collection of XL tees that I tuck into jeans four sizes too big, covering the entire shape of my body. I wear high socks and gold hoops, sweat suits and sneakers that speak for themselves. I no longer worry about looking *too* girly, or not girly enough.

I get to decide what makes me *me*, what makes me feel feminine or masculine, both or neither. And through this realization of choice, and its continued exploration, I see that I've never felt as attractive, as confident, and as sure in my body as I do now.

It's not over at all, this journey. In fact, for me, I feel it's just beginning.

Gender is made up,[66] but what *is* real is everything underneath our gendered costumes, the you that exists without any

---

66   It's a Western construct, something colonizing societies decided to force upon Indigenous cultures around the world since the fifteenth century.

of the cultural makeup on. The you that likes something simply because you like it, not because it's in the boys, girls, or "gender-neutral" section.

No matter our genders and how we choose, or don't choose, to identify, we deserve the freedom to express ourselves and to *be* ourselves. We deserve to heal from the colonization that's disconnected ALL OF US—not just women—from ourselves and our bodies.[67]

But in this current version of society and culture, we get lumped into the same conditioning, the same shaming, the same boxes that are meant to fit all of us at once, without any exceptions. Inevitably, we all fail to fit perfectly into them, and the implication is that it's *our own fault* for not being good enough. We're taught that being ourselves *hurts* the people we love. We're taught that being ourselves will be the very thing that makes us *unloved*. There's no model we're given for bucking the system and it working out.

Yet many Indigenous communities have historically had enormous space to integrate and celebrate gender variances (... before they were killed and colonized). Indigenous folks who embodied both masculine and feminine spirits were not only recognized but also in many cases revered as healers, visionaries, and medicine people. It was a literal *gift* for parents to birth these special humans with special powers. They were considered to

---

67   My queer fantasy very much includes straight men too! I want them singing out loud and walking in heels and getting up in drag at least once or twice. I want them to cuddle and cry and laugh so loud their bellies hurt. I want men holding hands and having picnics and baking each other cupcakes.

have "double vision," attributed to their ability to see through, and beyond, binary lenses. A fucking superpower indeed.

Today, trans and gender-nonconforming folks are doing the blessed work *every single day* to not only give themselves safety and freedom, but everyone else too. They are reclaiming their bodies, their power, and their pivotal roles in society from colonization. They are the role models. They are the leaders breaking all of us free. They are embodying this work and making the space for all of us to reap its benefits.

I am only *just* beginning to understand what my queerness means to me, how I want to wear it, live in it, wrap myself up in it. I don't have it figured out yet, and I don't think I ever will. To me, that's kind of the point.

If I'm practicing my queerness in the ways that I want to, then that means I'll *never* fit into anyone else's definition of [insert label here]. Which is scary but, even more than that, so freeing. I'm never gonna be a "good" bisexual,[68] ace, femme, whatever. My queerness, by definition, makes me undefinable.

Queerness is never an outcome; it's a process. Just like you are.

Queerness in and of itself is decolonization. It's deprogramming everything we've been taught and learning to listen to ourselves, our bodies, and our relationship to the world around us instead. It's releasing the need for answers and certainties, and creating more questions. It's a place to play, to explore, to

---

68   I use "bisexual" to mean attraction to the same gender as myself, as well as any other. There's another term I could use to describe myself, "pansexual," but I just hate it without any other reason than I don't like how it sounds.

forever discover new parts of ourselves. In queerness, there is never anything definite—dimensions, like bodies and identities, are all fluid.

That doesn't mean the process of coming into one's queerness isn't also violent. It can be a storm of shame, pellets as heavy as hail. It can take years, a lifetime, even a deathbed to step into. It always requires a death—a release, a letting go, a grieving of a you that you never were.

I still find myself grieving the version of life I thought I'd have back when I was a little girl in my dressing gown, my abuela reminding me to be ready for my prince. Back when I thought Hector and I were going to have babies and raise a family together, that all this was required for a happy life.

To let go of those ideas is to carve out every single reinforcement I was given of the path I was meant to lead, douse them all in gasoline, and throw a lit match on top of each and every one. Every step I make on my *own* path is a tiny death of the life I won't have.

And that's a miracle. Because I may not have the prince I pictured in my dreams, but I do have a prince that's even better.

Mine wears beanie caps as crowns and is building a king/queendom with me as an equal—and a lot of times not an equal, because they let me boss them around. ;)

They are not tall, dark, and muscular. They're short, soft, and supportive.

They swept me off my feet in the most extreme and unusual of circumstances, and my life and relationship to myself have not stopped changing since. And to imagine I almost didn't let them change my life because I didn't want to change so much—I didn't want to lose all I had, all I was.[69]

We must all be willing to lose in order to gain. We must grieve the lives we perhaps thought we were to lead and instead surrender to something much bigger than the fairy-tale stories we were told in school, at church, at home. We must be willing to hear our own gods clamoring inside our chests, squeezing our hearts until they can be released.

If I hadn't made it super clear yet, this journey isn't easy. Even full-blown queers, folks who've been out for a while and have confidently integrated their queer identity, have a hard time with this. Many still believe they have to be "*a certain kind of gay*" to be loved, to fit in, to be accepted by their own communities. Many still succumb to ideas about femininity and masculinity, who they should date and who they shouldn't, how closely they should resemble the cis hetero white supremacist patriarchy they (and we!) come from.

Bisexuals and nonbinary people fuck all that up in an instant, their sitting posture,[70] their spirits, and their closets everywhere all at once. They fully embody the meaning of queerness. That's not to say if you choose a binary you're wrong, or if you feel solid in one gender or another, one sex or another, it's less than. Not at all. I'm just sayin' there's a whole wide world of *everything* to discover, and if you can let yourself have a chance to dip your toes in whatever makes you excited, it's worth it.

---

69   Even though what I have now is INFINITELY better.
70   #PeakBisexualCulture is sitting "not straight" in chairs, according to the internet.

And it's not just bisexuals and nonbinary folks that carry visible and invisible identities—we all do. No one will ever know anyone just from a glance. And so we can't wait for the world to get curious about us. Instead, we've got to get curious about ourselves.

Once I started being okay with people not knowing me, I started being okay with really knowing myself.

We don't owe the world all of ourselves—we're allowed to take the time to reveal our pieces one by one. If someone doesn't want to take me for what they're seeing in the moment, and don't want to invest more time to know the rest, that's a *them* problem, not a me problem.

I'm uninterested in being projected onto like I've been my whole life by the straight world. I've got nothing to prove. I am queer, and that is enough. I don't have to have an undercut, or wear rainbow pins, or be anything other than who I already am. The ways I choose to engage with my identity, and my expression of it, is my own.

I recently went blonde—like, platinum. I got tooth gems and tattoos and started wearing glasses. I look a lot "queerer" now in how I present myself, even though I didn't make these choices for that reason. I made them for deeply personal ones in some cases, for superficial ones in others, out of necessity in the case of the glasses, and *all* for the fact that I've always wanted to do these things and felt I never could.

That's where the queerness comes in for me—not a specific aesthetic, style, or look, but rather the PERMISSION to do it.

To queer my body by recognizing that my body is mine and I can do whatever the fuck I want with it. That only I am the designated director of what it looks like, how it presents, and the things it does. I'm the only one whose opinion matters.

To get dressed and *not* think about men looking at me is a triumph. To choose a haircut because I feel like it, and not because it makes me look "hot" or "pretty," is an incredible release. To paint my body in the ways I wish—whether that's glitter on my eyelids or my brother's name tatted across my legs—is power. To redefine "sexy," and make it mine, make it new, make it *all of ours.*

None of these things has to do with who I have sex with or who I date—it's me with me, my queerness and I getting on the same page, becoming one, and even more importantly, becoming whole.

Bee tapped the syringe and inspected the needle. A few bubbles released, and the tip was prepped full of the thick, yellow liquid.

They looked at me nervously. "Can you shoot me up?"

A splay of color-coded tiny needles, gauze, and alcohol wipes were spread on the bed in front of us, after we'd spent the last half hour carefully following the instructions on the printed pamphlet, then googling it all again, just in case. I'd brought home cupcakes to celebrate Bee's first testosterone injection.

I looked at them, my body frozen in panic. I took a deep breath and shook it off—that needle wasn't going into me, so the least I could do was help Bee stick it into themselves.

Bee pinched a little section of fat on their stomach and I blacked out—but whatever happened, it seemed to have worked because by the time I came to, the syringe in my hand was empty.

As of this writing, it's been about six months of injections. Bee's voice has lowered, their hair has thickened, and their body has slowly started to change, almost imperceptibly to everyone else, but to me, it's like a thick curtain has been pulled off and now I can actually *see* my partner who'd been standing behind it. It didn't start with T[71]—this has been a journey Bee's been on their whole life—and their gender journey is not mine to tell.

My story comes from being a witness, and in many ways a participant, to the journey. My story comes from watching someone I love take dinosaur steps to come out—not to the world, but to themselves, which is always the hardest part.

Being the girlfriend of a transitioning trans person needs an entire book, because it is *not* easy—there's NEW hormones, new language, new desires, new bodies, new *everything*—but I feel like the luckiest kid in the world to be so front row to my partner's quest for happiness. *They* are the one who reminds me every day what it means to unpack it all for myself, who makes space for me to be all I am and all I want to be. They are the one who encourages my own exploration, who loves me in whatever I'm wearing, however I present. They push me to uncover and hold all the different parts of myself—not just the ones society told me were okay.

71　Short form for "testosterone," usually used in context of a transmasc person on hormone therapy.

The work that trans people do every single day is the same work that we could all be doing.

Trans people remind me every day that we are good enough. That I am good enough.

I don't need to fit in—at all, not even a little. And neither do you.

From my queerness comes my brilliance, comes my questioning, comes my curiosity. From my queerness comes my acceptance that not only do I *move* through the world differently than others do, but I experience it differently too.

My neurodivergence is the same kind of special that my queerness is, the same kind of different. They both come from the same seed planted right beneath my heart. I always felt it but never knew what it was, a sense of self clouded in confusion, until one day, clarity could burst forth.

Oh. I'm queer.

Oh. I'm neurodivergent.

I'm not wrong, I'm not broken, I don't need to be fixed. I'm just different, and always have been. This isn't a *bad* thing; it's a goddamn masterpiece of a thing.

I am *gloriously* me because of everything that makes me unboxable. I am gloriously me because there's no one else who can do me better.

So are you.

You don't have to do anything to realize your queerness. If you feel it, if you recognize it, you get to claim it all for yourself—whatever it looks like, whatever it is.

Whether it's visible or not doesn't make it any less real. Same goes with any other identity, which is why I bring up my neurodivergence because, yeah, not only has it been another form of coming out, of claiming, of understanding myself in a way that not necessarily anyone else can see, but also because, statistically, neurodivergent folks are significantly more likely to identify as LGBTQ+.[72] A double dose of blessings we get to have being in these neuroqueer bodies.

Whether you're queer and neurodivergent or not, you get to be you, all of you, always. You get to celebrate all your pieces and get curious about them. You get to find the joy in yourself where maybe before you thought you'd only find pain.

You get to rejoice in all your differences and CHOOSE to do so. And not just that, but you get to choose the family that not only accepts you, but full-on celebrates and loves on every single fucking piece of you too.

In fact, nothing is more queer than choice. The choice to live life exactly as you desire, surrounded by the people who know exactly how to love you.

For many queer folks, chosen family is a consequence of survival. Point blank. Many are rejected by their biological families completely, and others of us are just left unsupported and unseen. As queer people, we've done what we do best—make choices that give us the freedom and support to *actually* figure out what we need and get the support we deserve. We also learn to accept that non-chosen family can only do what they have the capacity to do, and the rest is up to us. It always is.

---

72   Hutchings, E. "Queerness & Neurodivergence: What's the Connection?" *XO Coffee* UK, October 4, 2022.

My chosen family is my center of gravity, a source of connection back to myself. The moment I found out my brother died, all I needed was to hear the voices of my friends.

It was one of the scariest things I've ever done, to call and say the most terrible words out loud. To call and to just fall apart completely. I did it because I knew I wouldn't survive this without them.

The day my brother was killed, one friend who lives across the world told me to send her pictures of my hands when I didn't have words. I sent pictures from the plane, from my bed, from the funeral.

Another one in Australia called every day until I picked up two weeks later, finally ready to have a conversation, then kept calling, even if I didn't pick up.

A third one sent me a weighted blanket from Tel Aviv, since she couldn't give me a hug herself.

While I was home with the rest of my (biological) family during this time, I quickly recognized that being around them was not the right place for me to heal. I also knew I couldn't be alone.

I needed my chosen family.

So I flew across the country with my puppy to where I knew I'd be held—my best friend Louise's house. On the trip there, the dog shit all over the airport terminal. He also shit in his carrier, shit on my lap midair, shit on the walk off the plane, and shit all over the bathrooms and hallways of SFO once we landed. His curls were glued together by his own poop, as was the jacket I was wearing. My pockets were lined with tissue paper covered in feces. For the eight hours of travel I cried and panicked, fearing he'd be taken away from me by police,[73] just like my brother had been. For the eight hours of travel I clung to his shivering, poop-covered body and refused to let go.

Once we finally (finally!) walked out of the airport, Louise, who had already driven two hours to pick me up, turned right back around to bring us to her home—shit-stained and all. And of course, the *moment* we got to her house, the pup pooped all over her expensive carpets too.

Louise feels like blood, like we were woven from the same pattern, dipped in the same dye. She is the other part of me, who I tell everything to, who sees me where I can't see myself. She's been there through every evolution, every nervous step— in darkness, and in light. She sends me postcards she's made herself, ships me books, passes along gifts in the mail. Without her, I wouldn't know who I am.

And she still loves my puppy even when he squats and dumps all over her house.

Louise has been so important in my queer journey, helping me take my first baby steps. She saw me and validated me before I even knew what to do with any of it, letting me find my own way to myself—and, just as importantly, letting me into her own journey of sexuality, showing me the way.

"Hey," I told her one day sophomore year of college, the snow falling in chunks outside. "I saw there's a Bi Group meeting happening tonight." Louise had just come out, and seemed to be struggling. "Let's go," I told her. "I'll come with you." I'd

---

73   "Ma'am, put the dog in the carrier. Ma'am, you will be on a no-fly list if you don't comply."

brought it up because I thought it might be helpful for her to be around others who could share in her experience. I wasn't going for myself—at least that's what I told myself. I was going for her, to support her.

After all, I was *such* a good "ally."[74] I'd started the first queer group in my high school's history, fought to make space for the voices that had never been heard where I came from. I volunteered and organized back home, working to change the Florida legislature[75] to support LGBTQ+ folks. Of course I was taking my best friend to Bi Group, crossing the campus bundled in sweaters and boots. I just hadn't yet realized I was going just as much for me as I was for her.

I've been there next to Weezy (as I call her) as she's fallen in love with women and gone through heartbreak. I've been by her side as she's gotten married and gotten divorced. I've watched her start a thriving queer pole community, a novel, and a new relationship. I've seen her through family shit and the deaths of her dogs. Meanwhile, she's been holding my hand through all of my shit—first queer kisses, a volatile mental health journey, sooo many different apartments, and the biggest tragedies I've known. She's watched me in my messiest moments and has fought to never let go.

Chosen family reinforces all that is wonderful in you. It allows you to show all your sides, the messy (and smelly) ones included. It is invested in, cared for, nurtured. It is spacious, imperfect, and sacred.

---

74 Lol.
75 Oh, Florida.

Just like any healthy relationship, it requires communication, some confrontation, and being comfortable with tension. It requires boundaries, affirmation, time invested. It is a living, breathing, ever-evolving thing.

Discomfort is okay, and even necessary. That's what makes it real.

I spent my early life doing everything possible to not have discomfort in my friendships, hoping that it could be a safe haven from all the discomfort I felt in every other kind of relationship dynamic I had. But as it turns out, it was way more uncomfortable to pretend and hide myself all the time. Pretending and hiding is precisely what kept me from having what I have now—friendships that are my medicine. Friendships that are deep, nuanced, intimate, rich. Friendships that I'm building a life with—even though I currently live thousands of miles away from each of them.

Most of us know, at least intellectually, that life is richer, fuller, and even longer with friends—and we'd be happier living closer to them (this is science![76]). But the reality is that instead, most Americans live within eighteen miles of their moms.[77] Most of us learn the hard way that Mom isn't necessarily the *best* person to get support from when in such close proximity, especially if we're building queer lives.

---

76   Matei, A. (2023, March 10). "Live closer to your friends." *The Atlantic*. https://www.theatlantic.com/family/archive/2023/03/neighbors-friendship-happiness/673352/
77   Bui, Q., & Miller, C. C. (2019, January 23). "The typical American lives only 18 miles from Mom." *The New York Times*. https://www.nytimes.com/interactive/2015/12/24/upshot/24up-family.html

And yet even a lot of us queer folks (and certainly straight ones) might be afraid to let our friends be family for real. Depending on a mix of privilege and our own family histories, we may not have stress-tested friendships the way we've stress-tested our blood family (or the families we were adopted by). It's socially acceptable to turn to relatives when we need to borrow money, when we need a job or somewhere to stay. But the queer concept of "chosen family" says otherwise. What would it mean to dig deeper into friendships-as-actual-support-systems?

Friends may be the family we choose, but that doesn't mean we're still not carrying around the relational baggage we picked up from the families we were raised by and the first early friend-ships we made. To make friends our family, we've still got to work that shit out and process it, learn to deal with and nav-igate it. Yes, we get to make the choice to surround ourselves with those who love and accept us for who we are and are will-ing to take the journey of life with us, but we've got to keep doing the work to make it healthy.

Which kinda begs the question: What *is* a healthy friendship? How do you define one for yourself? It may be helpful to comb through your current relationships and feel into whether your definition of a healthy friendship is reflected in any of them.

It can also be enlightening to look back toward childhood. How did friendship dynamics play out for you then? How do you think they affected your understanding of friendship today?

And of course, understanding where you want friendships to sit in the universe of your life moving forward is great information to have. Why do you want friendship, and what do you gain from it? What role does it currently play in your life, and what role do you want it to play?

Prioritizing friendship, if that's your goal, isn't a fairy tale. It actually means actively cracking the fairy tale of our Happily Ever Afters like an egg. It means being uncomfortable with doing life differently than others around us.

As much as there may be to poke at and deconstruct in Greta Gerwig's *Barbie* Blockbuster Blitz of 2023 (for another time), the biggest thing I took away from those two hours in a dark theater was the pleasure—and deep longing—I felt while watching the scenes that took place in the pastel-coated cul-de-sac full of open Barbie Dream Houses right next door to each other. Barbie would wake up and wave to Barbie. Barbie would be out on the lawn with another Barbie. Barbie would be making breakfast while Barbie was in the shower. Barbies were neighbors, best friends, and support systems for each other in this water-less, windless, hermetically sealed fake plastic universe.

And I want to bring that to the messy, germ-filled life outside of the Barbie-verse too. The Barbie Dream House cul-de-sac was a metaphorical, but also literal, representation of my dream—a world where I have my own space, where my friends all live within earshot in glittering plastic mansions of their own, where we are the support systems for each other in our daily lives. Not just weekly or monthly phone calls. Not just yearly visits. I'm talkin' every damn day in each other's business, every damn day on each other's lawns.

I want my friends to be sitting on the couch waiting to start the movie while I take a shit. I want to find them in my living room when I come home, a surprise because they just felt like it. I want to spend weekends making art together, going on walks together, sharing food we just made. I want to get into arguments and trust we can heal them. I want to feel their hands through my hair as I cry, and I want all our resources to be accessible to each other as we support, create, and expand this beautiful life we've made together, for each other, for ourselves.

This is what I want.

And as clear as it is to me, it's also scary, which makes sense. Maybe you, like me, have been afraid to tell friends that you want a life together, because you're afraid that that's not what they want too. We're *all* afraid to be rejected.

But but but—

We're encouraged to face all these fears in romantic relationships. We're encouraged to put ourselves out there and, finding someone we might want to build a life with, to move across the country, to commit to consistent communication, to invest—all with the same fear of rejection, failure, and intimacy we've just been talking about. It's actually expected of us.

Likewise, most of us are raised, and have no problem with, putting our blood families at the center of our lives—and we didn't even choose them. We're biologically or legally attached to these people, and therefore believe it's our duty to be there.

I vote that instead, we queer this shit and learn to use our chosen family members as emergency contacts. As our plus-ones to vacations, work events, and family affairs. As the fairy godparents to our children. As the safety nets to catch us when we don't trust that our own families will. We need them for small favors and big favors. We need them for movie nights now and our ninetieth birthdays later.

We need them.

And to me, this is what a queer life looks like—decentering romantic relationships as the key to happiness and flipping the hierarchy of relationship on its head. Friends are soulmates, family, and romance. I choose to put them at the center of my life, and I reap the benefits. It's because of Louise that I *eventually* came out,[78] that I quit a bad job, that I've had a place to stay whenever I've needed to get away from family. It's because Coco was there to hold my hand that I swallowed my very first SSRI and changed the course of my mental health journey. It's because of Meredith saying "fuck that guy" whenever I share something assholeish my dad does to me that I'm able to do something about it and show up for myself. It's because of Bryony and Natalie that I've taken the biggest steps to open up and be fragile, scared, and confused.

The right kind of friendships increase your lifespan (science![79]), but even more than that, they make living bearable when life feels really hard. They are a healing balm to lay over our bruises, the bridges, the stopgaps, the safety blankets of our souls.

They support us when we go home to visit family, they help pull us out of abusive relationships and situations, they

---

78   After years of her dropping ALL the hints that maybe maybe maybe I was queer?

79   Kim, E. S., Chopik, W. J., Chen, Y., Wilkinson, R. B., & VanderWeele, T. J. (2023). "United we thrive: friendship and subsequent physical, behavioural and psychosocial health in older adults (an outcome-wide longitudinal approach)." *Epidemiology and Psychiatric Sciences, 32.* https://doi.org/10.1017/s204579602300077x

offer a couch to sleep on when we decide to quit our toxic jobs. They're there for breakups and births and starting a business. They're there to cheer us on when we've fallen, to hold out a hand and help us get back up. Friends are the common denominator in being bad, because without them, being bad becomes too hard.

We can't be bad alone.

And, to be clear, this isn't just for queer folks—friendship is a psychological safety net for every single one of us, and without it we aren't humaning.

My *Barbie* Dream House Fantasy has had me investing in my friends like most people do their families—I book tickets, plan visits, have weekly check-in calls. We talk about long-term plans, how they'll fit together, how we can make our lives intertwine as much as possible. I do all this selfishly. I am better when I am with them. I live better when I am around them. I am not fully, *fully* myself away from them.

Humans are creatures of community, of belonging, of connection, and friendship is the stained-glass window our fullest selves can filter through, where all our selves are reflected in pieces, all the different parts of us that don't get to come out anywhere else. It's where the masks slip off, the belly hangs looser, and we can be tender and jagged all at the same time.

Each friendship is a unique print all its own; no two are alike. Some are based on laughter, others on depth. Some friendships connect over shared culture; others, over shared history. Like any relationship, they can get complicated as life changes and things ebb and flow. Like any relationship, they require investment, communication, intention, and care.

My friends, the close ones, the ones that are my bones, are dotted around the globe. I can't go to their houses for dinner or climb into their beds for a late-night film. Our time together is hardly spontaneous; it requires planning, an expensive plane ticket, stuffing a bag full of clothes for them to borrow when I'm there. This isn't enough for me. I'm greedy. I want it all.

So I've signed a lease for a year in a new country where I have a house with a garden and a big stained-glass window.[80] There's room for everyone to come visit and room to turn our home into a community center, a garden of connections for all the friends I've yet to meet.

I hope my Dream House Fantasy inspires you: to reach out more, to invest in your friends, to cry and laugh and be a brat in front of people who see you, who love you, who celebrate you for all that you are without having an agenda attached. Letting others in helps you be braver to further explore yourself and figure out who you are, what you want, and how you want to live.

It's because of my friends that I feel safe being queer, that I feel proud to be neurodivergent, that I feel loved and accepted exactly as, and because of who, I am.

I literally could not be me without them.

---

80   This is until Louise decides to have a baby and I help raise this child in the co-parenting communal life of my dreams.

You don't have to share my identities or my interests to make some of this stuff work for you. You get to shape and mold it however you like, paint it the colors that you love best. This is advice that can be foundational for *anyone*.

Step 1: Say bye-bye to the male gaze.

There is a whole wide world of expression, aesthetics, taste, and experience beyond straight men. Catering to them is pretty pointless unless you're actively getting paid for it. Cater to your own compass instead. What would you wear if you weren't worried about how "hot" or not you were to a dude? How would you style your hair, your choices, your entire life?

On that note, DUDES DO NOT KNOW BETTER THAN YOU. They might act like they do, they might tell you they do, but they don't. Ever.[81]

Ignore the mansplaining and consider how your relationship to your own opinions changes when you don't have dudes demanding you prove yourself all the time.

Step 2: Seek out spaces that are comfortable for you.

As a queer person, this might mean not being the only visible queer in a room. It might mean being in spaces where no one's looking at you sleazily for holding hands with your date or for wearing a top that shows your nipples.

If you're a neuroqueer like me, you get overstimulated easily. You get anxious in crowds. You panic if you're about to have plans without having *a plan*. Whether it's work, going out with

---

81   You might be a dude reading this, and it's still true for you too.

friends, or being with family, you have a right to feel good in your body. You have a right to speak up if you want to leave somewhere, if you require accommodations in any area of your life. It isn't embarrassing. It isn't needy. It's you making space for you.

Step 3: Make your friends the loves of your life.

I don't mean sexually, although if you're into that, go for it. I mean make your friends your family, your pillars, your home. Make your friends those you choose, and those who choose you. Buy them flowers, Venmo them for a surprise coffee, send them a letter in the mail. Romance them, talk sweetly to them, write them a song. Don't save all that shit for your prince charming, damsel in distress, or nonbinary king. Build a castle just for them.

DOMME

"The sweet-talking is not necessary [. . .] I am doing this because you are paying me, not because you charm me."

—*Valentine Glass*

I turned on the camera. I had no idea who I would see, but I was about to make good money from him. In my room, topless with hair past my shoulders, I wasn't trying to hide, but I was nervous. I'd never done this before. He hadn't either, and the moment he flashed on the screen, I knew he was even more nervous than I was.

I felt ready.

"Get down on your knees, hands on the desk," I told him. He just looked at me, fear flashing across his face.

"I said put your hands on the desk," I barked. He listened.

The more I stared at him, the more he twitched. His eyes cast down, avoiding me, his breathing quick. I ordered him to look back at me. He could only blink up for a moment.

"Does my body make you nervous?"

"Oh, Mistress. You're stunning. I'm terrified."

"Then keep looking."

Take a few minutes to write down the names of ten people in your life and all the things you could possibly ask them for. They can be big or small or anything in between—from a shiny new car to a scented candle. From asking them to do your dishes to rubbing your feet. Let your imagination run as wild as it can, horses galloping in the valleys of all your fantasies. When you get there, keep going. What else might you like? What else can you desire?

When you're done, look at the list.

Looking at what you wrote down, you might have an overwhelming feeling of pleasure, or of shame. Maybe both. Don't worry about it.

Without making excuses for any of the people on the list, what's stopping you from asking them for what you want?

Literally—what is stopping you?

It's just a question, a possibility to float out into the universe. You're just asking someone for something—they can say yes, or no.

For most of my life, I didn't realize I could do that, just want something, then ask for it. Especially from men. For most of my life, I'd made myself simple for them, keeping myself easy to fall in love with, patient and uncomplicated. I remained a soft place for them to land, to fall apart when they needed to. I'd turned myself into a mother, a teacher, a nurturer for countless men—and had enjoyed being those things for them.

It had given me a certain version of power, to see them small and vulnerable. But it never felt very powerful. *I* never felt very powerful.

So much of my early life was focused on doing everything "right"—being the good girl, the good girlfriend, the good student, the good daughter. The implicit cultural promise (still) is that women who are "good" are REWARDED—with respect, success, or simply being likable, which for women and girls is the highest prestige. So naturally, I'd believed that by being good, I'd be powerful.

But all that's a lie. It didn't make me powerful at all. In fact, it's precisely what took my power away, because the more I performed "good," the closer I came to someone *else's* power—men's, mostly—and never my own. I was giving them everything they needed to get a free ride to power, while I remained handcuffed in the backseat.

I realized that as long as I was adhering to someone else's rules—again, men's—my humanity, my identities, and my way of being would always be wrong. I'd never be good enough.

Anyone socialized to be a woman has been taught to be afraid of power.

In my family, my father instilled the expectation that I should fear his, and bow to it. My mother resented my power, my willfulness, and all the ways in which I didn't bow to her. My romantic relationships taught me all the ways power could be used against me, and work environments taught me all the ways in which my power[82] was counter to its goals.

---

82 Swap for "integrity" here.

We've all had individuals hold power over our bodies and our decisions, and it isn't just these personifications but the historical and generational structures they embody—the state, the patriarchy, white supremacy—that cause restriction, confinement, and obedience. In America, all bodies are navigating these systems, and if you're in a body that isn't cis, male, white, and heterosexual, you are most likely feeling their crushing weight all the time.

We are only taught the binary of power—you either have it, or you don't.

In society, most people in positions of power—meaning those who are in a position to affect others—aren't actually powerful.[83] Not at all. They don't know how to use the powers of power, and instead, they impose on others, believing that through assertion they will maintain it (Hi, Donald Trump, Elon Musk, Vladimir Putin, etc. etc. etc.).

In this context, when we think of the word "dominant," certain images might flash across our minds. It may very well be people who have had some kind of real control over us—a parental figure, a boss, a policeman. Disobey them and there are real, tangible, sometimes life-altering consequences.

And yet, power is a lot more fluid than that. It exists in every instance all around us. Every time we have a conversation, we're engaging in power dynamics (one person speaks, the other listens). Every time we step out in the world, we are either asserting, or dismissing, our bodies in space. Every time

---

83 They're not humbled with responsibility or confident with their abilities—instead, they stay greedy and insecure, inflating themselves with resources that are meant for the people their position affects.

we work with a client, or a manager, every time we walk into a store, we're engaging with power.

In this current cultural moment, it seems to be constantly reinforced that power is a "bad" thing because it means privilege, which also, according to everyone, is a "bad" thing. But privilege and power are merely energies that can be harnessed, and they can be used to impose on others *or* to lift them up. Having power and privilege isn't bad—it's what you do with it, and that can be its own kind of magic.

True power, the kind that can't be fucked with—by any person or institution—comes from having security and trust in yourself.

That's the kind of power I've always wanted. That's the kind of power I've always craved. And after a lifetime of being a prisoner to chasing proximity to fake power, I was ready to finally discover my own. It was time to step into my Being Bad Era, however shaky my first steps might be.

Just days after my relationship ended with Hector,[84] sporting my new bisexual bangs,[85] I wiped my post-breakup tears and put on bright red lipstick, gold hoops, and the shiny red fake-latex dress I'd just bought from some fast-fashion site, the one Hector had rolled his eyes at just days before. I was ready for my first party as a newly single person.

It just so happened to be a sex party.

---

84 Remember that? That was chapter 3.
85 And that was chapter 5 ;)

Come with me into the scene:

I've been writing and working with SexTech companies for the last few years, and so a lot of my New York friends are in the industry too.

SexTech has to do with all the technology built for the sex industry—from vibrators to digital sex ed products to contraceptives—but our community does things a bit differently. Almost all of us are in New York, and none of us are men. Everything we build and make is from a consent-focused and intersectional perspective for vagina-owners, which is entirely the opposite of how the traditional sex industry has been built. What we're doing is historically groundbreaking, and yet men won't stop hitting on us because our jobs have "sex" in the title, but because the "tech" is added . . . they think we're smart(?).[86]

Anyway, I'm in my fake latex for this party, the launch of a feminist porn magazine. The founder's a friend, and I'm going to wear this goddamn plastic dress to celebrate them.

As I'm strapping on my heels, I get a text from another friend of mine, a tall Polish actress who's always parked in the garden terrace of the Bowery hotel looking for people to invest in her "star-studded" film production company. Apparently, she'd been homeless. Apparently, she was coming into lots of

---

86 Can't even tell you the number of stories I have from female founders in pitch meetings with VCs where said VCs, almost all men in suits, make lewd sex jokes, ask them on dates, and try to touch them—in the meeting!!—instead of giving their businesses (a great investment, by the way) money.

money. Really, she's just another Anna Delvey with longer legs. I meet her at her usual spot in the lobby, and she hugs me.

"Congratulations, honey."

I look up at what feels like four stories from where I am to her face. Hector's just moved out, and I'm on my way to celebrate someone else's success, so what do congratulations have to do with me?

"Your breakup! You can be anyone you want to be from now on." Huh. I keep listening. "Your story's just beginning, babe. *You don't owe anyone a thing.*"

She squeezes me even tighter against her ten-foot-tall torso and turns to the crew of people next to her, offering to buy us all drinks in celebration. The grifter may be in her element, but it's still the best breakup advice I've ever gotten.

I decline the drink, give her another quick hug, and head to the venue south of Houston Street.

Madame X is all reds, velvets, and descending steps. Even the stairs that bring you to the second floor, where the event is, feels like sinking up into an intimate, cavernous dungeon space full of pulsing bodies, musky air, and thick energy. I'm nervous. I pull the bottom of my dress lower, hoping to cover something more than just my ass, but that only makes more of my breasts pop out. After pulling both ends up and then down, I give up and exhale, walking into the crowded space. My Polish friend's words repeat themselves in my ear. I can be anything I want to be.

I take a few tender steps into the crawling cell of the crowd and spot my friend Luna a few heads above everyone, as usual. Tall and angular with charmingly crooked teeth, she's gorgeous, intelligent, and always at the center of a party. Tonight's no different. I join her side and gingerly look around. I've never been in a space like this before. Some people are dressed as if it's a regular New York City night out, silk sleeves and short leather skirts, while others are in full fetish gear.

On my right is a woman in a latex leotard,[87] the glint of a zipper shimmering by her crotch and two tugging chains sprouting from her wrists. One is attached to a smiling, handsome man in underwear. He carries himself like a Shirtless Diplomat, walking tall behind his Mistress as if *he's* the one in charge. His gray hair and chiseled jaw confuse me. This guy's hot—I wonder why *he's* not the one pulling the leash.[88]

Looking at this couple, it's clear I've yet to understand the nuance of power dynamics in the way I am seeking. I still can't help but associate any kind of submission with weakness, and certainly something far away from masculinity. This will all change, eventually. For now, I look at them with a curious confusion, especially because there's a third involved. Another man, also in underwear, but with the addition of a black mask that fully covers his face. His leash is longer, and he's crawling on his knees behind the first two. In the categories of submissives, here we have a true slave.[89]

---

87 Real latex, the fabric squeezing every curve of skin, suffocating it deliciously.

88 Back then, I still had outdated ideas of gender roles and power dynamics, believing Hot Guy should be in charge. Sad for me (but not for much longer).

89 This is the BDSM terminology we use, although there's lots of cases for using it or not using it depending on your culture, body, and history. I use it here to differentiate between a "sub," who is submissive within a container, and someone who is fully, 100 percent in submission all the time throughout every interaction with their Dominant (consensually and with prenegotiated boundaries).

The woman leading this pack of men isn't conventionally pretty, so at first I don't get it. Why are these grown men completely bent to her will? I soon realize her power has nothing to do with the way she looks. This woman is somehow able to suck all the voltage of a space and pull it toward her, propelling everyone else to spin around her like a lightning rod, immovable at the center. She wears big curls, a hilly nose, and olive skin. I feel pride open in my chest. This power plant of energy is Jewish, like me.

The room is full, but as this Mistress[90] walks through the space, the sea of people part, a modern-day Miriam leading her men to freedom[91]—of a certain kind, anyway. Even through the throngs of people, I can't take my eyes off her. She tugs her subs across the floor and up the steps to a spotlit stage on the far left side, and I realize I'm not the only one looking. The crowd has leaned into her already, submitted themselves to a show that hasn't even begun. An iron railing wraps the front of the stage, and large curtains hang like cake batter ribbons from the ceiling, thick velvet pooling on the ground.

To begin the performance, Mistress Miriam pushes the Diplomat against the railing, his back pressing into the metal. She pulls the slave's leash in so that he's kneeling at the foot of the other man, and steps her seven-inch heels onto his back, a human footstool, as she buckles her strap-on, a curved purple dildo jiggling from her crotch.

---

90   There's a few different titles femme Dommes are commonly addressed by, but Mistress has always been my personal favorite.
91   Oops, another Jewish reference. Ya know Miriam, from Passover?

The room's already thick with heat, but now the quality is something slightly different. Sour and musky, nervous excitement leaking out of all our pores. Every single eye is on her, and she knows it.

Mistress Miriam hooks one of her stiletto boot legs over the railing, straddling the Diplomat, dangling her purple penis in his face. She yanks the slave's leash and brings him to standing, whispering in his ear and caressing his face. Then, just as quickly, she pushes him back down to the floor and turns her attention back to the man slammed against the railing. With a hand holding his mouth open and a tilt of her pelvis, she starts dipping her plastic crotch into his mouth. In and out, in and out, in and out.

I swallow. I want to grab Luna's hand, but I'm ashamed of my own response. I don't know what I'm watching or how I'm supposed to react. I feel small, unsure, and a little scared. Mostly, though, I feel silly. I know about kink and fetish spaces—I write about them all the time—but it's always been *theoretical*, something to think about, not feelings I've ever had to actually confront. I'm freaking out, but also entranced. Something about this mix of discomfort and terror feels good. Something about it is moving me, making me feel things that have nothing to do with my last twenty-four hours.

Actually, that's not true at all.

It's precisely *because* it's making me feel all the emotions from the last twenty-four hours of my breakup—a colorful cocktail of pleasurably terrifying uncertainty with a strong twist of pain—that I'm hooked. I can feel the grief, the shame of how hard I'd been holding on to a relationship that wasn't working, the exhaustion of always having to be in charge. And yet I can also feel freedom, the taste of not knowing whatever the fuck is going to happen next. I've never felt freedom in a relationship to someone else. I've never really surrendered to someone, or let them surrender to me. I'm terrified of vulnerability, of what it would actually take to let go.

These feelings feel Big.

Instead of shouting fifteen years of processing over this crowded room with music and the sounds of Mistress Miriam's moans blending in the background, I just catch Luna's eyes. They're as saucered as mine.

I turn back to the stage where Mistress Miriam's unhooking her slippery dildo and strapping it to the Diplomat's forehead. The slave is now licking the shoe she's standing on, his tongue running along her pointy heel, her leather boot, up the curve of her calf. She looks down at him as she begins unzipping the crotch of her leotard. She turns her attention back to the dildo, pushing the Diplomat's forehead lower. She's in a split, one foot on the ground being licked by the slave, the other foot now resting on the iron railing above the Diplomat's forehead as she positions her pelvis over his face. The purple cock disappears inside her as she begins to ride it, her ass smacking against his face every time she descends. I can see how hard he is from the stage, his smile visible every time he gasps for air. She doesn't touch him once.

I'm sweating. And confused.

I don't know why, but I feel uncomfortable and embarrassed for her. Her face is wide open in pleasure. So are her legs. Her pussy is visible to like, a hundred strangers.

And meanwhile, *she's fucking a forehead.*

The audience is going nuts, and I'm embarrassed for them too. They've completely lost themselves to her, animals howling in a sex-stenched room. It's too exposed, too strange. This woman onstage is powerful, but at this very moment, she's also small and soft and incredibly vulnerable. I want to be present with her here, this moment of *her* surrender, this moment when she gets to give in. But I can't help but feel uneasy, and then hate myself for it.

This point of the scene is intense, but mostly, it's tender, and when her body shudders, she lets out a low moan, immediately unhooking her legs. The tension in the room still hasn't broken, and she rips off the dildo from Diplomat's forehead and sticks it in his mouth, letting him suck off her juice. Here, I cheer. She grabs the back of his head and pulls him to the floor, making him kneel in front of the other man. She pushes their faces together and keeps her hands on their heads, standing over them as they take turns dipping their tongues into each other. This, too, surprises me in its tenderness.

I look down and realize I'm gripping Luna's hand, but I exhale when I notice she's gripping mine back just as tight.

With her leotard's crotch still unzipped, Mistress Miriam walks her men off the stage behind the curtains.

When I got home, I couldn't stop thinking about Mistress Miriam. Her performance was powerful, and I'd been wildly uncomfortable in her presence. I wanted to be like her—well, maybe not *exactly* like her, but I longed for the vulnerability, sensuality, and unashamed ownership of her power. After growing up with my father, my experience with my uncle and so many other men in my life, Hector, all my boyfriends, the president, the news—I was done being submissive to society, and especially to men.

I was ready to access my own power, and therefore my freedom. But I needed practice.

At the time of that infamous party, I didn't know anyone personally who was open about their kinky lifestyle, anyone I felt close enough to ask, so one day, sprawled across my bed's comforter, I typed "kink" into the app store, assuming there must be *some* kind of dating-style app for the subset, and picked what looked like the safest option. There weren't that many, which surprised me.

Once downloaded, I realized I couldn't browse users without making a profile. Fuck.

I clicked out of the app and tried to forget about it. Something about my curiosity felt dangerous, like I wasn't supposed to have it. I felt the flames of desire pulling me close, but kept feeling like any step I took toward that would somehow leave me covered in burns.

I hadn't even *done* anything about my kinky curiosity yet, and already I felt guilty. *Guilty of what?* I asked myself. Of wanting, of power, of wanting power. I took a deep breath. Fuck *that*.

I opened the app again. I was going to make a profile.

After I uploaded a picture—me by the sea, brown back exposed in a black dress, my face turned away, hidden by hair—the next step was to identify my role, but I had no idea what to pick from the scroll-down options. Domme? Mistress?

Goddess? What, exactly, was the difference? What, exactly, did being any of these things actually entail? Was I going to have to wear dildos all the time and change out my entire wardrobe for latex? Would I have to put away the soft parts of me forever?

I was desperate for the taste of power in that moment without having any idea what made me feel powerful.

I closed the app, terrified and excited, wondering if anyone would even respond.

Within minutes of my post, dozens of men had started writing to me, begging to serve, to be played with and fondled and yelled at. Men craving to give themselves up to me completely before I'd even shown them who I was.

I was confused. They couldn't even see my face, could hardly see my body—the things that had always easily drawn men to me. Here, it seemed, all that mattered was my Dominance, my confidence, my willingness to take these (self-described) weak men and turn them into *something* that might be of use to me.

I panicked. I giggled. I freaked out.

It was the first time in my life that I felt my power had nothing to do with my face or my body and that, perhaps, it had *never* had anything to do with those things, but rather everything to do with my attention, my energy, and my desires.

If only I could figure out what those were.

I wasn't yet ready to play in all the physically sexual ways these men wanted me to—I didn't yet know what cock cages were,[92] I hardly knew how to wield a crop—but I *was* ready to start practicing being in full control.

---

92   Which I now absolutely adore!

I started slowly, with things that I *knew* I loved and desired—like books and social justice.

I had men order works like Inga Muscio's *Cunt* and Roxane Gay's *Bad Feminist*. I had them write book reports, follow activists online, and comment their support. I had them working to unlearn all the things I couldn't make Hector, or any man in my real life, unlearn or listen to me about.

At first, it felt good. I had them doing what I told them, had them eating out of my hand. But then it felt empty.

Nothing that I was doing was really about me and my desires. It was about what I thought would benefit *them* and *their* growth. This wasn't what I wanted to practice nor what I was here for. I was here to have my fantasies fulfilled.

I didn't just need submissives—men who were consensually agreeing to my control in a specific container in order to have *their* fantasies fulfilled—I needed full-on male slaves. Men who were so submissive that their *only* desire, their *only* fantasy, was to please me, no matter what it was.

I didn't yet know what my Big Fantasies were, but I started playing with some small ones.

I had my slaves make me dance videos, buy me little things I liked. They did arts and crafts with pictures of my face, creating little altars by their nightstands. They bought plants and cared for them by singing songs praising me. I had them do things for me I had never before believed I deserved to ask for, had never realized I even wanted.

It was playful, childlike, and unlike what I'd seen any other Domme ever do, but it felt right for me.

I still didn't want to play with these men sexually. That eventually came later, after I'd done an incredible amount of work to get clear on my own boundaries and desires and discovered that, actually, the idea of depriving a man of ejaculation, of watching him sweat and squirm, of feeling his desire for me and calling it weak was actually fun *for me*. But right now, I was here to figure out how I could come back to myself, discover who I really was underneath all that I'd been taught about how to relate to men.

How I could ask, demand, take up space.

How I could go after what I *actually* wanted, not what I'd been told my whole life to want.

How I could release any ideas, expectations, or pressure to be any other kind of powerful person than exactly what I was already.

But even as I was stepping into my power, into my Domme-hood, I was still struggling to release control with the image I had of what a "good Domme" should be—always in control, no signs of vulnerability, and having all the answers.

One night, I woke up sticky, sweat staining my bedsheets. I had dreamt that my slave had left me because I wasn't a *real* Dominatrix—because I didn't wear latex suits or have my hair in a sleek ponytail. I had never yelled at him or made him kneel on a bed of nails. I didn't even have long ones—nails, that is. I was *too* nice, *too* easy, not demanding *enough*. The things I made him do were stupid, he told me (in my dream). What kind of Domme requests book reports, plant videos, and daily affirmations? His face blew up into an angry hot air balloon as he floated away.

After catching my breath and realizing it was all in my head, I almost started crying before I started laughing.

I *knew* that being in power *actually* meant being comfortable with surrender, being vulnerable, and admitting to not having all the answers. I knew it was about integrity, honesty, and gentleness when needed, hardness when helpful. Slave and I had a deep bond—we were in communication constantly, building a connection unlike anything I'd experienced before. He loved how I Dommed him, and I loved all I was learning in doing so. The kind of relationship we had, and the trust that existed there, was what was powerful—not the outfits I wore.

I got to decide how I dressed and how my Dominance expressed itself. No one could tell me how to do that—not society, and not him.

It scared me how easily I had almost fallen back into the "good girl" trap I'd just climbed out of, even if now, on the surface, it looked different. How quickly I could slip back into believing that I had to please a man.

Even as he kneeled before me and called me Goddess.

Even as he prostrated his body and called me his Queen.

This wasn't just going to take a few months of practice to undo. Releasing everything I'd internalized to be "good" would take a lifetime. But here I was with a human slave at my feet, a man begging for my power to be expressed, and I was ready to see it for myself.

With all the practice I was having, I was getting really good at being in my Domme energy. I was onto something; I could feel it. And I knew it had nothing to do with sex itself, but all the things sex represented. The tension, the power, the energetic connection, the presence it required. How I could twist a man's intestines with my gaze, drop him to his knees with a single word (literally). How I could have things bought for me, my house cleaned for me, wake up to affirmations of my majestic beauty, just because that was what I wanted that day.

I began offering space to folks who wanted to learn what I'd been learning. It felt important to me to create an environment where others had permission to explore their power and pleasure in their *own* ways. Sex can be a traumatic place for so many of us, rather than an implicit place of pleasure, and yet we *all* deserve to benefit from the lessons of power and desire, regardless of whether we're engaging in anything explicitly sexual or not.

Never before had I believed I deserved that. I was finally learning that I did.

I was also learning that I could make money off of my attention. Quite a bit of it. I'd never felt so respected as a woman, as a wage earner, and as a worker.

After years of working in toxic New York City advertising agencies and start-ups, and years of being rejected and belittled for writing and speaking in the SexTech space, what I was doing as a Domme felt *different*.

A few years before, I'd moved to New York City for a dream job at what was the most inclusive newsroom in the world at the time, on the eighty-fifth floor of One World Trade Center. I ran their feminist channel, doing celebrity interviews, producing viral videos, and creating an audience that *cared*. But in the end, as often happens in capitalism, the company's wokeness was just a façade, and all of us "diverse" hires just felt used and exploited; all the while plenty of not-so-woke things kept happening, things I felt every day while working there. Anyway, it didn't last long. I was let go five months later, in a surprise mass layoff affecting sixty other employees, during the media industry's scramble to "pivot to video."

The thing with having your dreams given to you, then taken, while in One World Trade Center is that you can't go a single place in the city without seeing it. Everywhere I went, there it was. Everywhere I looked, it stood beaming up above everything, the sun and sea reflecting off its phallic presence in blues, pinks, silvers, and golds.

When I looked at it, it reminded me of all I'd fought for, and all I'd lost. It reminded me that I was no longer receiving gift packages, or invitations to events, or people wanting my attention. It reminded me that my ideas, my perspective, even maybe *I* was just too much for anyone to want.

I struggled for a few years, to say the least.

I went through multiple rounds of experiences like this one. Workplaces that promised change, inclusivity, a mission to make the world better. Roles with titles I'd never thought I'd have, clients I'd never imagined. But every time, around the five-month mark, something would happen. Usually, it was me being let go.

"You seem to have bigger aspirations," said one CEO when I was doing my job *too* well. "I know you'll just leave us. So might as well do it now."

"You're clearly not a fan of the way we do things here," said another, after I'd asked to talk about homophobic remarks and actions she'd made toward me and other employees.

"You're brilliant," said a third. "We know you'll find your way, it just won't be here."

It's really easy to blame a toxic workplace once . . . but when every workplace starts feeling the same, the next logical step is to blame yourself. I kept feeling like I was too out there, too naive for believing that the workplace could be somewhere I could be respected.

Of course I'm not the only one who's felt this way. In fact, most people with marginalized identities in the workplace do.

A study published by Coqual (formerly the Center for Talent Innovation)[93] found that 76 percent of Latinos report repressing parts of their personas at work. This includes everything from modifying the way they dress to changing their body language and communication style. For most of my career, I've been one of them.

I have many identities; femme, queer, Latina, and neurodivergent are just some of them. While my body—and anyone else who has a body with a uterus—is constantly being con-

---

93   Center for Talent Innovation. 2016. *Latinos at work: Unleashing the power of culture.* https://www.talentinnovation.org/_private/assets/LatinosatWork_Infographic-CTI.pdf

trolled by the state, the traditional workplace does the same to my ideas, emotional labor, and attention.

These are workplaces that *still* pay me less than men; workplaces that, in a majority of states, can still legally discriminate against Black hairstyles; workplaces that allow 85 percent of autistic college graduates to go unemployed;[94] and workplaces where almost half of LGBTQ+ workers experience discrimination.[95]

After having had so many traumatic workplace experiences, in a rather self-affirming realization, it suddenly became so obvious to me that *I* wasn't the problem. I'd never been the problem. The system and culture these workplaces were operating in was.

Our entire society is built upon this system, and most of us can't actually just "walk away." But we *can* make different choices, ones that are right for us—even if it means walking away from where you are *now*. It feels important to acknowledge that an enormous amount of privilege exists in these decisions. It's not possible *for so many of us* to just quit, or leave, or be without health insurance or a steady paycheck for a while. And yet even so, we all deserve to be in places where our bodies feel safe and relaxed. We are allowed to walk away from a toxic workplace in search of a better one.

---

94   Pesce, N. L. (2019, April 2). "Most college grads with autism can't find jobs. This group is fixing that." *MarketWatch*. https://www.marketwatch. com/story/most-college-grads-with-autism-cant-find-jobs-this-group-is-fixing-that-2017-04-10-5881421

95   The Williams Institute at UCLA School of Law. (2023, February 14). *LGBT people's experiences of workplace discrimination and harassment*. Williams Institute. https://williamsinstitute.law.ucla.edu/publications/ lgbt-workplace-discrimination/

Through sex work, I found a better version.[96]

I explored different avenues of the trade, eventually landing on virtual Domme sessions and some occasional cam and photo work. I commanded respect from my clients, not just in the way they greeted me—"Yes, Mistress"—but also in the way they paid me. Unlike in my life as a professional creative, invoices were paid up front and never delayed. My expertise was never questioned and my unique knowledge was not whittled down to numbers on a spreadsheet. I was thanked profusely by my clients for simply being me and all that I was in my power. I didn't feel used. I felt their gratitude, their appreciation, their relief. I refused clients who didn't align with me, and I built relationships with those who did.

For most of my career in the creative industry working for others, I'd been treated terribly. I was great at what I did, and bosses and creative clients knew it, so they tried to squeeze as much out of me as they could. In sex work, it was different. Men tried, but I was already coming in hot from the get-go. They were coming to me *because* of my power, and the moment they undercut it, they lost all access.[97]

Consent, power dynamics, and safe spaces all require the same ingredients no matter the meal you're trying to make. My macro view of current professional, cultural, and social land-scapes is due to my civ[98] experience, but as a sex worker and space holder, I've also got a micro one. Sexual domination—

---

96   To be clear, not a *perfect* version. A better one—especially because I was privileged enough to choose it and not need it.
97   Boy, bye.
98   "Civilian," aka non-sex work.

just like domination in the real world—can take many forms. Actually, domination play directly riffs off of the power dynamics and oppressive structures that we all live under daily. That's kind of the whole point—it allows for a space to redefine the shit we've been through, the shit we don't understand, the shit that's hurt us, the shit we like.

Sure, we're talking about sex here, but not in the way we've all been taught.

I've held the hands of many as they've stepped into their journey to reclaim and redefine their relationship to their bodies, to their jobs, and to themselves. It's all related. It all comes from the same place.

We all have a relationship to dominance—it's often where most of our trauma comes from. We also all have a relationship to anger. It lives inside us, whether we acknowledge it or not. We all have violence we'd like to exert, and some of us even have violence we'd like exerted *onto* us. Instead of understanding that this is normal, healthy, and *only to be expected* living in a violent society that forces us to repress so many pieces of ourselves, we are taught to internalize it all. We believe we are the only ones who feel this way, believe we are broken because of it.

It's not true.

We aren't taught how to relate to these parts of ourselves, and when they do come out—as they always, inevitably, do—it's often in not very safe ways. Kink spaces allow for the practice, the release, and the experience of engaging in and creating a *new* relationship to those parts that we may have once believed were never allowed to come out.

So the only thing left to do is to realize that we are already perfect as we are in our imperfection, in our messy, strange, animal bodies.

As a Domme, I have worked with women, trans men, and nonbinary folks wanting to be Dominant in the bedroom. I've also worked with cis men, trans men, and nonbinary folks wanting to be submissive and serve. The kind of healing, play, and space I've offered hasn't been available without looking at how each individual shows up in the rest of their lives—*outside the bedroom.*

As a space holder and sex worker, I could give anyone an hour of release, of pleasure, of distraction—and that's valuable—but what I really wanted was to give folks the tools to continue exploring, integrating, and playing with those pieces themselves. I never wanted them to need me. I wanted to give them the space to figure out what they needed so they could get it without me, and keep going.

Although trading tit pics for hundreds of dollars from guys online was quite lucrative, I paused, wanting to invest my energy in others who were just as dedicated to their journeys of healing their relationship to power as I was.

At first, women came to me because they wanted to learn how to be Dominant in bed with men. Often, we mistake the root of something as having to do with sex, when really it's about everything else that surrounds it.

These women came to me seeking tools for partner play, but ultimately, they were sitting in front of me because they wanted more power over their own lives, because they wanted to stop giving their power away—to their bosses, boyfriends, children, and parents. They needed support in figuring out how to step back into the power that was theirs and protect it, removing anything that was in their way. And they needed a framework where it would be safe for them to do it.

I worked with trans folks who were beginning their transitions, or who were fresh on the other side of it, and found a space with me where they could slowly step back into their bodies, learn the new ways it could move and feel, and discover all the new desires that were sprouting in their systems. I had them dance for me, sing for me, slow down and move gently as I sat giving orders on the other side of a screen.

I had men who wanted access to their feelings and who hired me, ultimately, to open their clogged and clotted emotional channels.

For any human, sex can be an incredibly vulnerable and exposing place. There's weird noises and sounds, sweat and smells that spill out of our bodies. Many men, having internalized truly useless (and dangerous) messages about masculine sexuality, repress the possibility of this sexual vulnerability that would require, in some way, "feminizing" their approach to intimacy and actually participating. So instead, they find comfort in playing out the powerful aggressor, the one in control, dictating and owning the experience. Been there, done that (remember toe blood guy?[99]).

---

99   Chapter 3.

The dudes coming to me still believed these messages, but they were beginning to break away from them. They'd already gotten in touch with the part of themselves that knew there was something much deeper for them to experience than superficial sexuality if they were willing to let go. Once they were able to open up and submit themselves to an experience—in this case, a sexual one—often, they would find it much easier to open themselves up emotionally in the rest of their lives as well. Sometimes that involved me dictating an experience of sexual release for those who had a hard time feeling confident. For others, it meant denying them of it so they could learn to surrender without using sex as a performative crutch. Everyone needs something different.

Here, I was a witness, a container, a space to practice without judgment, without fear.

People call me a sex and relationships "expert" because of all the work I've done in that space, but really, I just deal in the hands of emotional labor and intimacy[100]—I'm a question-asker, a dot-connector, and an avid practitioner of my own hypotheses, which means my conclusions are always shifting based on context.

I don't have truths to offer! I don't have ten quick tips to try!! And there will certainly NEVER be a one-size-fits-all response that I give!!! There will always be others far better equipped than I am to tell you how to give great head or structure your polyamorous relationships.

---

100 As long as the intimacy isn't turned on me . . . jk I'm working VERY HARD on that.

My interests have always lain in how someone's showing up to the sex, to the relationships, to themselves. I'm curious about how they're feeling while they explore what's between their partner's legs—or don't—and what they're doing to lean into the pleasure of it all. The logistics, to me, are relevant, but totally secondary.

Plus, the tease, not the consummation, has always been what excites me the most.

"Mistress, I'm so horny all the time." This was my youngest sub, a man in college who was struggling to focus on his exams.

"From now until finals are over, you'll wake up, and instead of masturbating"—here was the catch—"you'll do thirty push-ups. Redirect the energy. Record yourself, and send me the videos by 9 a.m. every morning."

"Yes, Mistress. Thank you, Mistress. I'm such a stupid, embarrassing, disgusting boy."

"Yes, you are. And because of that, you'll buy yourself a cock cage, stuff yourself in it, and only have access to touching yourself when I say so."

Easy. Problem solved.

We must examine and deconstruct "sex" as a concept, an act, and a tool. What does it mean to have sex and to experience it, and how can we learn to define it *for ourselves*?

We must look at what it means to be in a body—the control and confusion we've experienced, but also the freedom. We must look at how the intersections of capitalism, colonization, ableism, racism, transphobia, and fatphobia have informed the relationship we have to our identities, our bodies, and power. We must look at our bodies in context—the moment in time we find ourselves in, the moments that came before, and how we relate to all of it.

We must also confront the pleasure, desire, and *want* most of us have been categorically denied, allow ourselves to grieve their historical absence, create new maps and pathways to get there, and ultimately get *it*—whatever "it" represents for each of us.

Power play is all about subverting the societally enforced power dynamics that we have no control over and flipping them onto their heads. Maybe that's gender roles, maybe that's trauma, maybe it's religion or finances.

If there isn't shame underneath to work with, I'm of the belief that it won't be very fun, and it can even be dangerous. Playing around with power, especially when you've got marginalized and oppressed bodies and identities involved, requires an enormous amount of care, intention, and respect. Nothing has to be off-limits as long as everyone agrees to it and feels safe, held, and excited about it.

The funny thing is that folks who spend their days out in the world full of control (CEOs, white men, religious patriarchs) are often the ones seeking places of surrender in the bedroom. The folks who have been forced to submit all their lives (anyone marginalized, but here, especially, we're talking femmes) get quite the kick out of taking the reins. But in the bedroom, depending on what you like, it can switch again, and there's nothing wrong with that. If you want to stick to your gender roles and amplify and play with them in a conscious way, hell yeah. But you've always *always* got to understand the other role (and always *always* be aware of the fake Dommes that roam the internet looking for newbies to take advantage of[101]).

The best thing for a Dominant to know how to do is to truly surrender. If you don't know what it is to feel safe and release, how can you offer that to someone else? If you don't understand the bravery it takes to open yourself up completely, how can you demand that of another?

Meanwhile, the best thing for a submissive to know how to do is to take control. You can't be a healthy submissive without understanding what your boundaries are, without knowing how to assert yourself, without knowing how to communicate. To throw yourself and your body into a situation without safety isn't correct. It's disrespectful to all you are. To be a submissive takes as much work as it takes to be a Dominant.

The experiences I was having during this time, and the decisions I was making, might sound extreme to most people, and they felt that way to me too, even while I was in them. In no way was I confident or even comfortable during my initial explorations. I felt *way* out of my depth, like an imposter snooping in the land of the free—but that's what I wanted. To be free. And playing with power was my map to get there.

Contrary to what most of us were raised to believe, power isn't some static, immutable, ownable thing. It's a dynamic—it's

---

101 NEVER give your power away completely! Your trust is to be earned, not expected.

contextual, fluid, and based on a relationship. Dynamics can shift and be recalibrated and reoriented in an instant.

If you take away all the external things that seem to make someone powerful—whether that be money, resources, status, or identity—what's underneath is just a person, a person who has vulnerabilities. When a person really owns those vulnerabilities, that truly makes them powerful. True power is a full embodiment of spirit and a shamelessness of self. It's the ability to be seen and to see others.

However, wanting power for power's sake isn't powerful. Power is there to serve, to take up space and be humble at the same time. That's not the kind of power we're taught to aspire to, or have role models for, or are given the skills, resources, and space to practice.

All of us find ourselves in various dominant and submissive roles throughout our lives. Every time we engage in any kind of exchange with another, power roles are activated, and there's a chance to play with them.

Power dynamics are all about who gives and who receives the attention. Any time you take attention off of you and flip it back to whoever just gave it, you're being a Domme.[102] Any time you're able to take yourself, and the personal, out of a situation and call the shots from that gently removed, clear place, you're being a Domme. You are grounded, rooted, unswayed by whatever's happening outside of you. You respond to it, but you don't react. You are brave and unafraid of silence. You make your request and demand it with your body, with your atten-

---

102 I'll keep using the femme term "Domme" to generalize.

tion, with your gaze. You do not speak to fill the gaps, do not overexplain, do not prove. You simply are—and you know that *that* is the greatest power there is.

It gives me a childlike joy to intentionally employ my Domme energy in dynamics where someone else is trying to, perhaps intentionally, but certainly unconsciously, Dom me. I've had grown men with incredible power fumble their words, lose their train of thought, completely unfold in nervousness before me. And many times, this hasn't even been during a Domme session—this has happened in conversations with executive producers, hedge fund managers, and big-time lawyers. They all put their attention on me thinking I'd shrink. Instead, I put it back on them when they weren't expecting it, and they were the ones who came apart.

All I did was ask a question. All I did was not look away.

Today I'm rarely stepping into my full-on Domme because she's much more integrated into who I am all the time. She's there when I'm writing emails, when I'm negotiating pay, every single time I say no. She's with me whenever I need her because I now know I *am* her. Sometimes, when I'm feeling far away from her, or like I need a reminder, I strap on my boots and walk around with a whip—but these days, that's usually only *inside* the house.

Now that I've found this energy, it's important to keep nourishing that relationship. It's never something to take for granted, especially because most of us aren't given tools to reconnect with our power in the first place, or to show us how to access it. Instead, we're taught to be at constant war with ourselves, our internal trust broken and meant to be replaced with other things outside—like promotions, nice cars, a tight butt, a bestselling book. We're taught to play a part and let nobody know we might be struggling so we'll be taken seriously. We're taught that we'll be powerful as long as we can play god to all the puppets in our lives. But the reality is there is nothing in the outside world that can give us what we need to give ourselves on the inside.

Because here's the thing: True power and freedom actually have everything to do with submission and nothing to do with domination.

It isn't in the performance, it isn't in the presentation, it isn't in the projections—it's in the willingness to allow for things to get messy, uncategorized, changed. It's in the willingness to fail, to fuck up, to acknowledge it and do better. It's in the willingness to be "found out," discovered, unmasked. If we're always trying to hold on to control, it's because we don't trust ourselves to be in an unknown situation. If we're not willing to let go, it's because we're scared of not knowing what will happen to us, and we don't trust our own ability to navigate it.

I found that to practice a holistic, honest, and higher Dominance, I had to become familiar with the authentic—and often uncomfortable—process of submitting to the complexity and messiness of myself.

You can be into spiritual things or not, and the thing for you can have whatever name you choose—your higher self, Love, God, the Spaghetti Monster in the Sky, whatever. The point is, it's not the Ego You that's powerful, the You that wants to control, boss around, and manipulate out of fear. To access your power, you actually have to surrender to the Openhearted You, the Soft You, the All-Seeing, All-Powerful You that rules with a gentle hand (and sometimes a stinging slap).

As a Dominant, it is always your job to remember that it is your submissive who holds the ultimate power[103] because they are the only one who can tell you how far you can go. They can decide to stop at any time or ask for more. The Dominant is there to hold it all, to find the delicious edge but never push past it. To play with rejection, with shame, with fear. It's pretty sacred work.

In these dynamics and relationships, no part of ourselves is left behind. Here is where our shame and confidence coexist, where our sadness and joy intermingle.

Getting in touch with my inner Domme has been the greatest source of power and connection back to myself I've had, on a personal level and on a professional one. It was because of my Domming that I had the freedom and the push to leave a very fancy but toxic job (thanks, OnlyFans cash!). I didn't leave that job to pursue sex work and Domming full-time by any means— those are jobs like any other, with stressors and boring bits, but with the added weight of being extremely isolating and lonely

---

103 In a play scene, but also if we're talking about work dynamics or parenthood or anything else with clear power roles. Ideally, the person "in charge" needs to understand that what they're there for is to hold and support the experience of the people that aren't. That's the only way they can be a good Domme.

due to society being *stupid*—but I was really grateful for all I'd learned, all I'd received.[104]

I'd spent so long worried I'd be found out, worried I'd be unhireable should anything ever leak. I was so concerned about what others might think of what I was doing that I hadn't been grounding into what the experience had actually been like for me. It'd given me a chance to level up in myself, and I didn't want to hide it anymore. I didn't want to hide *any part* of me anymore.

What I wanted was to keep working in the creative and entertainment industries—I'm a creative director and writer, and those are the places where I can do what I do best—but it needed to be on my terms now.

So in July 2022, I posted "sex work" as a work experience on my LinkedIn. My intention wasn't to start an international commotion. It wasn't even to start a conversation around sex work at all. That part was almost irrelevant.

I wanted to shine a light on the hypocrisy that is "professionalism" and the corporate capitalism this country practices. I wanted to show how fucked up it is—how sexist, racist, and *white* it is. How objectifying it is. How violating. (I didn't have to do much; the commenters on my posts did all that for me.) I'd been treated *far* better by clients in sex work than by *any* client or manager I'd had working in civ jobs. I'd been listened to, respected, and paid appropriately, unlike at any job where I'd held some fancy title. In sex work, I can protect myself a lot

---

104   I've had the enormous privilege to enter and exit as I please, something I'll never take for granted.

better because I know what I'm getting into, and therefore I have power. With agencies and start-ups, it's all a slippery illusion that makes it much easier to fall into, and therefore have none.

In a world that loves to flatten us, wants to turn us into one-dimensional paper dolls, I choose to be human.

I made the post to take the steps I needed to own all the parts of me and publicly celebrate them. It is all these parts—where I come from, what I've lived through, the things I've done—that make me who I am, that make me so good at what I do.

The post made international headlines for weeks. My face and name were plastered all over major news publishers and broadcasters.

I hadn't asked for it. I hadn't intended it. And the point was never to be the global face of the sex work positivity movement—there are people far better equipped to handle that than I am. All I wanted was to stop hiding from myself and the world.

But let me tell you, this whole moment-in-the-spotlight experience exposed a lot of things to me.

1. It showed me how unsafe American workplaces are for most people, how bigoted and dangerous. There are managers, employers, HR reps, and CEOs of companies who had no problem shitting all over me publicly on a professional platform. They projected their morality, called me names, and wished me terrible things—all in the name of "professionalism." Did they get fired, lose clients, have a single consequence for treating me the way they did? Nope. They are protected by the status

quo, by power, and by the rules they themselves made up and continue to reinforce.

2. From my act of self-ownership came the entire world wanting to own me too. People from all corners of the world felt entitled to my attention, my story, my body, and my bank and social accounts. I was hacked multiple times on multiple platforms and had to change all my cards. I received lewd and unwelcome messages and solicitations through every medium and had to take down and hide family pictures and email addresses, no longer able to access any space that had once been mine without someone else trying to take it from me.

3. And because, god forbid, a woman makes a decision for herself, everyone seemed to want to involve my family. Journalists copied my father on emails about the story (LIKE WHAT), and different members of my family each received full multipage printouts of these published articles with a personal letter that strung half-baked sentences together referencing my partner (my "trans pimp," apparently), me ("your whore of a daughter"), and all the "shameful, disgusting" ways I was "an absolute disgrace to [my] family." There were a lot of people invested in trying to shame me into submission.[105]

4. Everyone was obsessed with figuring out what kind of sex work I did.

---

105 Cute of them, but it didn't work.

Despite the point of my post being to highlight my many dimensions, the world had flattened me into the "LinkedIn sex work girl" anyway. I've had to learn to shake it off and be okay with most of the world not knowing who I really am. I mean, after all, did they ever?

Ultimately, taking the steps to own all of myself has led me to where I've always wanted to be—writing books, working on projects with creative agencies and brand clients who trust and respect me, and working in the ways that are best for my brain, body, and spirit. I now make money precisely *because of* who I am and the full spectrum of experiences that I bring to the table.

My best work doesn't come from putting me in a box; it comes from giving me the box and then letting me smash it wide open to create something different.

I know that now, and so most days I feel pretty successful. Not by anyone else's standards, but my own.

Most of us think being free is a way of being, but it's not.

It's a choice. An active one.

And all I want for you is to be free, on your terms.

So forget everything you think you know about being Dominant. Everything you think you know about being a slut, a certain gender, a partner, or a boss. I want you to release all the ways in which being any identity isn't serving you, come up with your own ideas, and take your power back.

In this current moment, when our rights are being stripped all over the place, when our voices are being silenced, and when our bodies are being controlled, I want you to look at the decisions *you've* made, the ones you've had control over—your job, your friends, and your relationships—and ask yourself, "Do I want this?" If the answer to any of them is no, then I want to know, what *do* you want?

It's time to explore your *own* version of power.

Exploring your Dominance literally means exploring it exactly the way you want to. Exploring what makes *you* feel vibrant and alive, not what makes someone *else* feel powerful, and certinaly not what society says is powerful.

It doesn't have to look like a CEO title or an Amex Black Card in your wallet. It doesn't have to look like whips and floating sex chairs. It doesn't have to involve any sex—or any executive roles—at all. In fact, it absolutely shouldn't until you're excited and tingly at the prospect of consensually telling someone what to do, centering them and their care throughout the experience. Dominance is not something to be pushed into, it is a choice to step into, and one that requires you to hold your vulnerabilities and your confidence all at once.

There's a million and one different ways to express power, and the only one that should concern you is the way that you do it. It's a lifelong practice, the way most of the things in this book are, but one that is oh so worthwhile.

It's quite literally life-changing. I've had clients quit careers, get promotions, end marriages, find the loves of their lives. They've moved countries, transitioned their bodies into their gender, and found their real voice to speak from.

This shit works.

What it all comes down to, what this book—but really, this life—is about, is that you are in complete control of you, of who you are and the choices you make in this world. Yes, society, upbringings, cultures, and institutional oppressions affect us. Yes, they *turn us* into who we are. But they are not who we are, and they don't get to make choices for us. Only we do.

This lifelong (if not longer) process is about learning to trust YOU, and not any other voice, not any other person or system. It's about remembering that you have a unique power all your own, made just for you, and it deserves to be grounded and moved into spaces where you'll shine.

It's also about not giving a fuck what anyone else thinks.

We're here for two seconds, if we're lucky. What are you going to do with it?

Being a Domme is all about taking your power back, and Being Bad is all about reveling in it.

Maybe it sounds easy for me now, like I've got it all figured out. But you've read some of my story and have seen firsthand how truly uneasy it all has been. It's *still* not easy. It's still scary and uncomfortable and sticky.

Reader, as you probably can guess by now, writing this book was a series of hot messes for me. I was drowning in the grief of losing my brother, but also from the inane pressure I put on myself to make something perfect, worrying what you would think, what my parents would think, what ex-boyfriends, future publishers, past collaborators would think. But even more than that, I was worrying about what *I* would think—and for the most part, I didn't think a lot of it was very good. All the mental and emotional Band-Aid crutches I'd used throughout my entire life to get me through hard shit just didn't work anymore when the hard shit got too hard. I was being undone at the seams, and so I had to learn to ask for help (which I did![106]). But, even more than that, I had to learn to be okay with where I was, and what I could make, even when it wasn't perfect.

And so this is not a perfect book.

While writing it, I had moments of anger, of hope, of despair. Moments when I was struggling to believe in anything anymore, moments when I was finally ready to challenge and laugh at myself again. If I were a Good Author, I might've changed each chapter for maximum consistency and narrative flow. But for *Being Bad*, I decided not to.

I decided to be a Bad Author who's (finally!) okay with leaving things imperfect—because I've learned that nothing perfect is ever good, and nothing good is ever perfect.

I had to learn to take my own advice and be willing to surrender to the process, to this moment in my life, and to this beautiful creation that I gave so much of myself to (and to stop trying to control everything![107]). I had to learn to figure out my desires, my boundaries, my rituals, and my navigation of rejection of my own self to get here.

So here's some ways that, maybe, you too can take Domme energy and integrate it into your own life, achieving what you want—and even more than that, celebrating and falling in love with yourself—along the way:

---

106 You'll see in the acknowledgments!!
107 MUY hard for me.

1. Set your own boundaries and desires.

Boundaries and desires go hand in hand. Exploring what you like, what you don't, and what you *might like* but aren't yet ready to explore is imperative. I'm not just talking about sex here— I'm talking about everything.

The moment we start setting boundaries—not with others, but with ourselves—we are stepping into our power. Boundaries are not for others; they're a commitment to ourselves. We can't control anyone else. We can't set a boundary and make them follow it. What we can do is decide what our *own* boundaries are, communicate them, and take action for ourselves if they are crossed.

A boundary I have looks something like this: If someone raises their voice at me, I will communicate to them that I will not continue the conversation until they soften their tone. If they continue, I will remove myself from the conversation. I can't *force* someone to lower their voice, but I can do something about whether or not I'm present if they don't.

People who have gotten very used to you *not* having boundaries can be disoriented once you start enforcing them. They may call you selfish, unhelpful, a disappointment. They might turn you into the villain.

Can you enjoy playing this new role?

It can feel delightful to disappoint. There's a visceral pleasure that can come from knowing that you're acting in ways that precisely feed *you*. That you actually owe no one anything, that you can luxuriate in the space-taking that every witch under the sea and on land seems to know so much about. You don't have to play nice anymore—you can just play yourself.

Villains know what they want and they stop at nothing to get it.

What do you want?

2. Once you know what you want, learn to ask for it.

This is about embracing the reality that, like my father always says, "You don't ask, you don't get."

Even if you ask, it doesn't mean you'll get, but you certainly won't get anything if you don't ask. This is about reminding you that you can always ask, and you don't have to take whatever response you get back personally.[108] You can take it in stride. You can take it as play. You can take it as a lesson.

There is a whole wide world to put yourself out there in front of, and it's simply a disservice to the magic of the experience of being alive to not move toward all the things you want.

3. Get comfy with rejection.

Which I am terrible at, by the way. All the more reason why it's so important for me to keep practicing it, keep working through it, and keep redefining my relationship to it.

A major reason why we don't ask for what we want is because we're afraid someone will say no to us. And yes, that no is tied up into so many things—it's not just the no we're afraid of, but the vulnerability, the exposure of desire, the worry that we'll be

---

108 As someone with ADHD and rejection sensitivity, this one's extra hard for me, but practicing it has made all the difference.

unloved. But, in the end, a no is just a no! When you zoom out, it's a pretty silly reason not to go after something.

We can't practice asking if we're not practicing being okay with rejection. When we ask for something, we are not in control of what the other person will say. We also can't expect an immediate yes; otherwise, what's the point of asking in the first place? We might as well demand.

With asking, there's a playful air of curiosity, a liminal space full of potential and possibility. We must be okay with not knowing until we receive an answer. Likewise, we need to be okay with whatever the answer is. If you don't like the answer you get back, keep the playful energy going.

4. Don't shut down.

This can be the hardest part—it certainly is for me. Upon any kind of rejection, my go-to is to protect myself, get defensive, and lock up my feelings. But that's not very Domme-like.

Instead, if something you've asked for has been rejected, see if you can stay curious, stay calm. Remove the personal. Pay attention to the feelings, but see if you can put them aside. Expand into considering why you weren't met with a full-on YES.

If you get a no, can you ask another question? Can you ask, "Why not?" Can you ask, "What would turn that into a yes?" Can you ask, "Where is the no coming from?"

Whatever you can do to keep the conversation going, to keep the other engaged, *this* is where the Dominant energy truly thrives. No matter the context, no matter the answer, there can be a calm, cool, confident Domme unbothered (but still listening and paying close attention to non-verbal cues[109]) by whatever someone else is saying, unruffled by rejection, understanding it's just an opportunity to continue the game. It's not about being perfect; it's about learning to enjoy the mess of it all.

Own your desires, own your inner Domme, and watch the world fall to their knees before you—metaphorically, and if you so choose like I did, literally.

5. Connect with your own roots.

So much of our "unwellness," and therefore our smallness, has to do with our disconnection, from forgetting that we are part of something so much greater and deeper and bigger than just . . . ourselves. Domming is ultimately about surrendering yourself to that bigger thing—the universe, God, your highest self, the Spaghetti Monster in the Sky, whatever you want to call it. Stepping into your power (and then playing with it) is so much about having access to that ultimate power—not outside, but within yourself.

Go through old family photo albums if you have access to those. Do some research on your lineage and the cultures of your ancestors. See what you can pull from them, and see what you can use to further play and pray with.

If you don't have a connection or know about your genetic lineage, make up your own! Choose some ancestors. Ask them to guide you. Learn about their foods, their customs, their

---

109 Domming is never an invitation to not center consent. Quite the opposite. You can play, as long as the other is playing with you.

prayers, their ceremonies. What does their language sound like? Their songs?

This is about creating a connection to practices deeper and older than you, but not taking them directly or without questioning them. It's about relearning to ritualize and create your own ceremonies. To bow at the altar of your own beliefs, not someone else's. Take inspiration, take connection, then make it yours.

6. And finally, do whatever the fuck works for you and your body.

You deserve to feel comfortable, to feel safe, and to be pushed to grow in ways that feel good. That's real power right there.

Explore, discover, and listen to the cues of your body and your nervous system, just like you would do with a sub. Practice surrendering and submitting to yourself. Learn what you need to make yourself comfortable; learn when you need to speak up when you're not.[110] Make the world accessible to you; make it enjoyable. Ask for the accommodations you need. Give yourself aftercare when you've gone through an experience that pushed you or made you tender; let your body bloom underneath your own touch.

Move toward the spaces, people, and practices that hold and accept and love you as you already are. It's only from there that any true healing, and true power, can happen. It's only from there that any of us can be well.

---

110 That's what you'd expect from a good sub, and you've gotta put it into practice for yourself first.

You don't actually need to change a thing about yourself. Accept that first. Hold that first. Then go off and take any steps you'd like to make you feel even better. Not be better, just feel better.

There's a difference, and it's big.

EPILOGUE: BEING BAD

> "I am doing my best to not become a museum of
> myself. I am doing my best to breathe in and out."
>
> —*Natalie Díaz*

I take a deep breath, listen to the soft guitar strings I hear from the main house, feel the breeze from my open window, hear the clip of paws on the wooden floors. If my nose weren't stuffed with snot, I'd be able to smell the magnolia flowers, their perfume bright in the dusk. My office is the garden studio in an old house, the windows ancient, one clamped shut from the vines. I can't open it, and yet a vine has snuck in, like a tentacle reaching toward its future. Its leaves are just as sprightly as its siblings' outside, and I wonder if there's a lesson for me there.

My heart is clamped shut like that window since my brother died—I can see through it, the garden, the green, the view—but I can't feel it, can't fully participate in it. And yet, inevitably, an arm from the outside forces itself in, reminding this room—and my heart—of life, of possibility, of continuing to grow even in the most unlikely of places.

My heart's an empty room with its windows sealed shut, and even as I'm trying to figure out how to open them, life comes in. Nature comes in. It continues to fight to survive, continues to overtake whatever's there. It will never stop growing.

And neither will I.

You can't be bad and be afraid of grief.

To be bad is to be in constant grief, to mourn so much of what you've known in order to become who you are. It's a leap of faith that you never fully land on, a flight that lasts forever. It's a burying of expectations, of old patterns, of versions of your life that are no longer alive.

It's painful. It hurts. It's disorienting. But the release must happen in order to make space for all that's coming. For all you've chosen, for all you will continue to choose.

Every morning I wake up with ants in my chest, a stampede of legs crawling between my breasts as they dig beneath my skin. My body buzzes with all the possibilities of the day—not particularly positive ones—then gets paralyzed with fear. Within thirty seconds the ants descend into my stomach, where they become snakes that take over my intestines. They spend the day slipping through my organs, sometimes sliding all the way back up to swirl in my brain.

I've suffered from my stomach my whole life. Abuela used to tell me it was emotional, but that was back when my dad had told me anxiety was a weakness and depression just a mindset. I didn't believe her.

"Trust me, Ariellita," she said. "I had that same kind of stomach pain too, and it was the day your grandfather and I divorced that it went away."

She also told me about my great-grandmother Abuela Blanca, who made the best chile relleno and bourekas on the island, cooking huge feasts every day for lunch. Right after the table was set, as all the men ate, she'd climb into bed and shut all the curtains, where she'd stay until the next morning. She suffered terrible migraines, but they were miraculously cured the day her husband died.

I think about all the grand legacies of the men in my family, names on buildings and factories, history books and birth certificates, and I think of the bodies of all the women beside them—silently suffering, their stories still left untold.

I think of the Holocaust, the way it always chases my abuela, and—I realize—the way it always chases me. I've spent my whole life attempting to shutter my mind's eye from the scenes I see, the visions I feel, the truth that exists in all of them. Every generation my family has fled. I'm the first that hasn't had to, and yet I feel chased out anyway, by my insides, forced to escape myself, constantly leaving a piece of myself behind.

There's a lot of trauma in my body, but worse than that is the trauma of *being* in a body that fights itself, a brain that terrifies itself, a system so sensitive it would rather just watch so it won't have to feel.

I've spent years floating above myself, just looking so I wouldn't have to participate. I had no idea how I got there, and I was desperate to bring myself back down.

I've climbed volcanoes barefoot, gone days without food and water while sleeping outside, and swam miles in open ocean with my bikini top slipping off. My body is strong, capable, and resilient. It's the everyday living that feels like a marathon, improbable and impossible.

I can hook my knee on a pole and twirl upside down, stand on my hands, and do as many sit-ups as you ask me to, but to walk into a room full of people, to feel what they feel, to feel what I feel—I hide it all, well enough, beneath my skin, beneath my smile, but being alive hurts.

For most of my life I thought I was a monster, then I thought maybe just everyone was. I've learned that it's neither, that life hurts for some more than for others, that there are other people who also hurt like I do. I've learned it's not something to abandon, to ignore, to run away from. It's the relationship I make with it that turns me into who I am.

To be ashamed, to wish I was different—I understand why. It's something close to hell just to open my eyes most days. It wasn't always this way, but mostly, it was. To pretend I can escape it isn't helpful. To know I can dance in it is what makes it possible, is what makes space for the laughter, the smiles, the joy. There's so much death in my body, all I can promise myself is to keep moving toward life.

The songs that make me sway my hips, the breaths that smell like the garden in my backyard, the way my dog feels on my skin. The hands I hold that bring me warmth, the coffees I drink that focus my mind, bring me peace if just for a moment as I write a poem, string together a sentence, craft some medicine with my tongue.

I'm not a monster for being in a body, my body. I'm not a pervert for existing with my brain. I am a human, an animal, a piece of earth shaped into muscle and skin. If I try to trap myself, I grow sick. It is with acceptance, compassion, and claws full of rage that I become fully me.

It is not through following a certain style of dress or manner that I escape. It is not through my credit score that I manage. It is through placing my hands in dirt and my feet on bark that I remember. It is through baring my stomach and cutting my own hair that I express. It is through bleeding past my bedsheets and digging my fingers into skin that I scream.

For years I pretended to smile, and for years after that I screamed to forget. Now I do my best to practice silence. I make subtlety my teacher, the only master to bow down to my own truth.

I take up space, but it is my own. I speak words to show, not hide behind. I stumble and slip and do my best to surrender. It doesn't always work—I hold on too tight, refuse to let go—but eventually, I see there's no other way. There's resistance and then there's living.

I choose to live.

It can take me a while, but I choose it. I can stay in bed for days over it, but I choose it.

Living means letting parts of me die; it means putting pieces of me to rest. And still, I know, I must choose it.

The alternative is living a version of me that's *already* dead. One without growth or a future worth having. One that keeps moving through the haunted houses of fear.

To live *means* to die too. To choose life means to kill off what will inevitably kill us if we don't let it go.

Don't ask me to tell you how to do it gracefully; in fact, don't ask me to tell you how to do it at all. I don't know. It's simply a choice.

The word "decide" has the same root as "homicide." To choose is to kill every other possibility.

It is a violent act to become.

We enter this life pushing through skin and covered in blood. We enter this life surrounded by screams.

Living can be no different. If it is not that, it is not a life.

Become. And keep becoming.

ACKNOWLEDGMENTS

Thank you, dear, beautiful, brave reader. Without you, this book couldn't exist.

It also—literally—couldn't exist without Bee. This is their book too. Bee put in as much work into this as I did, and on top of that, put up with the *insufferable* human I was for the months I was writing (I love you). They also didn't let me quit (neither did my brother). I tried, more than once.

To my siblings that are still here with me: Natalya, Levi, and Megan. Everything (everything!) I do is for you, and because of you. Being your oldest sister is what makes me who I am.

To my soulmates: Louise, who spent half her vacation drinking coffee in slippers and editing chapters on my couch (and who is my soul reincarnated into a best friend that wears matching pajama sets with me), Natoosh for combing through my words with such care (while holding my hand as I take the steps to open up, teaching me I'm allowed to be loved for me), and Bryony for letting her phone storage fill up with years of crying, laughing, desperate, and ecstatically hopeful videos of our faces, showing me that I can give my heart to someone and have it be safe and loved. The greatest gifts I've had. I'm me because all of you. Estrella too. Through this process I've been shown how intimidatingly brilliant my friends are. I am so lucky. Thank you for loving me, in all of me. Meanwhile, and just as importantly, Coco for letting me cry and laugh with her in every language—our own language—wherever we are in the world (and for sharing her bonne étoile, *and* for taking my pantsless author photo), Tobias for being a text and a sauna away, and all my people—Kristen, Maddie, Meredith, Joamir, Jord, Helen, Bril, Aly, Ale, Ari, Berel, Baba, Tio + Diego, Abuela, and so many others—for all being pebbles of support, and sources of joy, in this life. Tex y Taki, por salvarme la vida, todos los días.

To the professionals: Lauren, for stuffing me with fancy sushi and wild dreams, Lynn and Cara for believing in this project (and me) from the very first moment, leaving little love notes along the way. Dara for saving the mess of my brain in a pinch, and Maya and Karen for scraping through it all with a fine-tooth comb. Pamela for chasing me in the visions I had for the cover, and Jessica and April for being the fairy godmistresses to get this book in the hands of the world. There are *so* many Jewish women who dug their hands into the earth of this book, and I swear it's all extra blessed because of it.

Thank you Books & Books Miami Beach, for being my first home, and my parents for always buying me printed worlds and doing the very best they could. And thanks SSRIs. Couldn't have done any of this without you.

LOVE YOU all. For real.

xx

CORALIE LAVERGNE

Arielle Egozi's work is centered on the destigmatization (and celebration) of all bodies, brains, and identities.

She is a creative director, brand builder, and strategist partnering with brands and agencies to bring a nuanced cultural perspective into their work. They also sit on the board of Do the WeRQ, a nonprofit highlighting LGBTQ+ voices in advertising. She is a 2023 PUENTES fellow, a university guest lecturer and creative industry mentor, and *Salon*'s inaugural sex and love advice columnist. Her writing has appeared in publications such as *NYLON*, *Business Insider*, and *Teen Vogue*.

They have spoken on stages around the world and have been featured globally across major publications for her taboo-breaking work. She shares a bed with her two perrhijos and partner.

Her weekly newsletter, "Bad Taste," exposes thousands of subscribers to artists, designs, and curations from around the world, and you can see it all if you follow her—@arielleegozi on LinkedIn and Instagram. But seriously, follow her. She won't survive TikTok or whatever other new thing will be out by the time you read this.

 www.arielleegozi.com   @arielleegozi